Philip Hewitt

Mein Erfolgstrainer
Englische Grammatik

Englisch 7/8

Klett Lernen und Wissen

Bibliographische Information Der Deutschen Bibliothek
Die Deutsche Bibliothek verzeichnet diese Publikation in der Deutschen Nationalbibliographie; detaillierte bibliographische Daten sind im Internet über http://dnb.ddb.de abrufbar.

Auflage 4. 3. 2. 1. | 2011 2010 2009 2008
Die letzten Zahlen bezeichnen jeweils die Auflage und das Jahr des Druckes.
Dieses Werk folgt der reformierten Rechtschreibung und Zeichensetzung. Ausnahmen bilden Texte, bei denen künstlerische, philologische oder lizenzrechtliche oder andere Gründe einer Änderung entgegenstehen.

Internetadresse: www.klett.de
Zeichnungen: Ergo, Stuttgart (Dieter Weiss): S.13, 23, 44, 53, 55, 59, 75, 94;
Katja Wesner, Fellbach: S. 52, 95, 107, 121
Umschlaggestaltung: know idea GmbH, Freiburg, mit Franziska Döhler
Satz: Klaus Bauer, Bondorf
Reproduktion: Meyle + Müller, Medien-Management, Pforzheim
Druck: Media-Print Informationstechnologie GmbH, Paderborn
Printed in Germany.
ISBN-13: 978-3-12-927137-6

9 783129 271377

Hallo liebe Schülerin, hallo lieber Schüler!

Dein Erfolgstrainer ist genau das richtige Buch für dich,
- wenn du dich in **einem bestimmten Thema verbessern** möchtest
- wenn du dazu **Regeln, Übungen und ausführliche Lösungen** in einem einzigen Buch suchst und
- wenn du wissen willst, wie du **deinen Lernstoff zeitlich am besten einteilst**.

So erstellst du dir dein persönliches Aktiv-Lernprogramm!

Im Inhaltsverzeichnis stehen links alle Themen, die behandelt werden. Rechts werden die Themen zeitlich eingeteilt, damit du dir **dein ganz persönliches Lernprogramm** zusammenstellen kannst und dann sofort siehst, wie viel Stoff du in welcher Zeit erarbeiten kannst.

Lerneinheit: Eine Lerneinheit beträgt 20 – 30 Minuten. Das bedeutet, dass du die Übungen in dieser Zeit schaffen kannst. Aber: Das ist nur ein Richtwert. Wenn du am Anfang länger brauchst – auch kein Problem!
Eine Lerneinheit solltest du an einem Stück bearbeiten. Wenn du 2 (und mehr) Lerneinheiten machen möchtest, ist es jedoch besser, eine 10-minütige Pause dazwischen zu schieben.

Tag: Wie du im Inhaltsverzeichnis siehst, verteilen sich zusammenhängende Themen manchmal auf mehrere Tage. Versuche, an einem Thema dranzubleiben. Wenn du z. B. montags anfängst, bearbeite dienstags die nächste Lerneinheit! So bleibt am meisten hängen und du musst nicht noch mal von vorne beginnen.

Woche/Monat: Wir haben den Lernstoff zusätzlich in Wochen und Monate eingeteilt, damit du sehen kannst, wie viel Zeit du insgesamt für größere Kapitel benötigst.
So hast du immer den Überblick und bist auf den Punkt genau vorbereitet.

Wir wünschen dir viel Erfolg.

P.S. Mit deinem persönlichen Aktiv-Lernprogramm kannst du dich ohne Stress auf deine **nächsten Klassenarbeiten und Tests** vorbereiten.

1 *Simple present* oder *present progressive?*

Hier wiederholen wir den Bedeutungsunterschied zwischen *present progressive* und *simple present* und üben die richtige Anwendung der beiden Formen.

1.1 Der Gebrauch des *simple present*

Wann benutze ich das *simple present*?

Diese Form wird verwendet:

1. für Einzelhandlungen – besonders Gewohnheiten –, die bisher regelmäßig in der Vergangenheit ausgeübt wurden und vermutlich in der Zukunft ausgeübt werden – nur nicht gerade im Augenblick.

   Signalwörter (Häufigkeit): never, always, sometimes, often, seldom, rarely, every day/week/month/year usw.

   He **is often** late home.
   He **always cycles** to school.
   We **rarely go** to Brighton
   She **visits** me **every week**.

   Achtung: Achte auf die Stellung der Häufigkeitsadverbien im Satz: vor einem Vollverb, aber nach dem Verb *to be*.

2. für Gewohnheiten längerer Dauer, Gefühle, Vorlieben, Abneigungen, Besitz usw., die keine Einzelhandlungen sind:

   She **lives** in Glasgow.
   I **love** ice-cream.
   They **own** a big house.
   He **hates** potatoes – he **prefers** rice.

Dear Pen-friend,

My name is Pat and I live in Carlisle. Carlisle is a town on the border between England and Scotland. It's near the sea. My family – my parents, my little sister Cindy and I – live in a small house near the town centre.

My mother works at a supermarket. My father is a bus-driver. He hasn't got a job at the moment. There is a lot of unemployment in our part of Britain and it is difficult to find work.

I go to the local comprehensive school and my sister goes to the junior school next door. My hobbies are skateboarding, swimming, football and playing computer games. What kind of sports do you like?

My full name is Patricia, but I hate it and everyone calls me Pat. I don't know your name because this is my first letter to you. Our teacher says she will send all our letters in one envelope.

I hope that your letter is a bit longer than mine! Tell me where you live, what you do in your free time and something about your family.

Yours,

Pat McLaren

1

Mache zwei Spalten und ordne die Sätze des Briefes zu:

Simple Present (einfache Form)	**Auxiliary Verbs** (Hilfsverben: *be, have, can* usw.)
I *live* in Carlisle.	My name *is* Pat.
…	…

2

Was kannst du über dich und deine Familie oder deine Freunde sagen? Bilde zehn Sätze.

My Uncle .../Aunt ...	lives	
I	work	to ...
My brother(s)/sister(s)	works	at ...
My mother/father	go	in ...
My best friend	goes	
Some of my friends	live	

3

Setze die in Klammern stehenden Wörter in die Sätze ein.

1.	(ever)	Do you go to London?
	(often)	We go to London Airport to see the planes. And what about you?
	(every week)	We go shopping there.
2.	(never)	We buy "The Sun".
	(always)	But "The Times" is very interesting.
3.	(rarely)	I have time to read a daily newspaper, but
	(sometimes)	I buy a weekly paper.
4.	(regularly)	Do you go to a disco at the weekend?
	(seldom)	I have time – especially at the weekend.
	(often)	At the weekend I go to the cinema.
5.	(every day)	Does she walk to school?
	(often)	No, I see her at the bus-stop.
	(always)	She takes a 49 bus to town.

4

Ergänze die Sätze wie im Beispiel. Vergiss die *s*-Endung bei *he, she,* und *it* nicht!

Beispiel: "I go to Windsor Comprehensive School." – "What about your sister?"
"She goes to Windsor Comprehensive School, too."

1. "We live in Windsor." – "What about your Uncle Jeff?"

____

2. "Jenny goes swimming every Friday." – "And Paul?"

____

3. "I like ice-cream." – "What about your brothers?"

____

4. "They play football on Saturdays." – "And you?"

____

5. "My teacher speaks French." – "What about his wife?"

____

6. "I often do the washing-up at home." – "And the cooking?"

____

7. "Jean plays the piano well." – "What about her friend Sheila?"

____

8. "Melanie and Jason fly to Spain for their holidays every year." – "And their mother?"

____

9. "Patrick cleans his room every week." – "And his bike?"

____

10. "The cats often sit beside the fire." – "What about the dog?"

____

1.2 Der Gebrauch des *present progressive*

Wann verwende ich das *present progressive*?

Diese Zeitform wird verwendet:

1. für Handlungen, die gerade im Augenblick passieren.

   Signalwörter: now, at the moment usw.

   She **is watching** TV at the moment.
   John isn't here. He**'s cycling** to school.
   Look, the bus **is coming**.

   Beachte die Schreibweise: sit – sitting; come – coming

2. für Handlungen, die in einem längeren gegenwärtigen Zeitraum ablaufen und als vorübergehend empfunden werden.

   Signalwörter: this year/season/week, at present

   Michael **is working** in London this year.
   This week my sister **is speaking** English all the time with our guest from England.

   (Das *present progressive* kann auch verwendet werden, um zukünftige Handlungen auszudrücken. Näheres dazu findest du in Kap. 6).

5

The new boy

"Who's that new boy in your class?" "You mean Christian? His name's Christian Meier. He comes from Germany but his father is working over here in England for a year. He's a teacher at our school." "So where is the family living now?" "In the house where the Jenkins normally live. Mr Jenkins, our German teacher, is working in Germany for a year. He and his family are living in the Meiers' flat in Dresden." "I see. Does Christian speak good English?" "His English is quite good. He only speaks German at home, of course, because hardly anyone at our school learns German, worst luck!" "Why? – Don't you like French?" "French is OK, but French grammar is difficult." "German grammar isn't easy, either. We're learning German at our school. All those endings! It's terrible!"

"Well, Christian says that English is easier for him than Russian was." "Did he have Russian at school?" "Only for one year. Then they changed to English. Why don't you come to the youth club this evening. You can talk to Christian there." "Good idea."

a) Trage alle Sätze aus dem Text, die im *simple present* bzw. im *present progressive* stehen, in die jeweilige Spalte ein. Sätze mit Hilfsverben (*to be, to have* usw.) lässt du bitte aus. Kürze die Sätze ab (z. B. *"Does he learn English?"* statt *"Does Christian Meier learn English at school?"*).

Simple Present	**Present Progressive**
…	…

b) Schreibe kurz auf, warum die einfache Form oder die Verlaufsform benutzt wurde.

6

Sieh dir die Bilder an und schreibe auf, was gerade passiert:

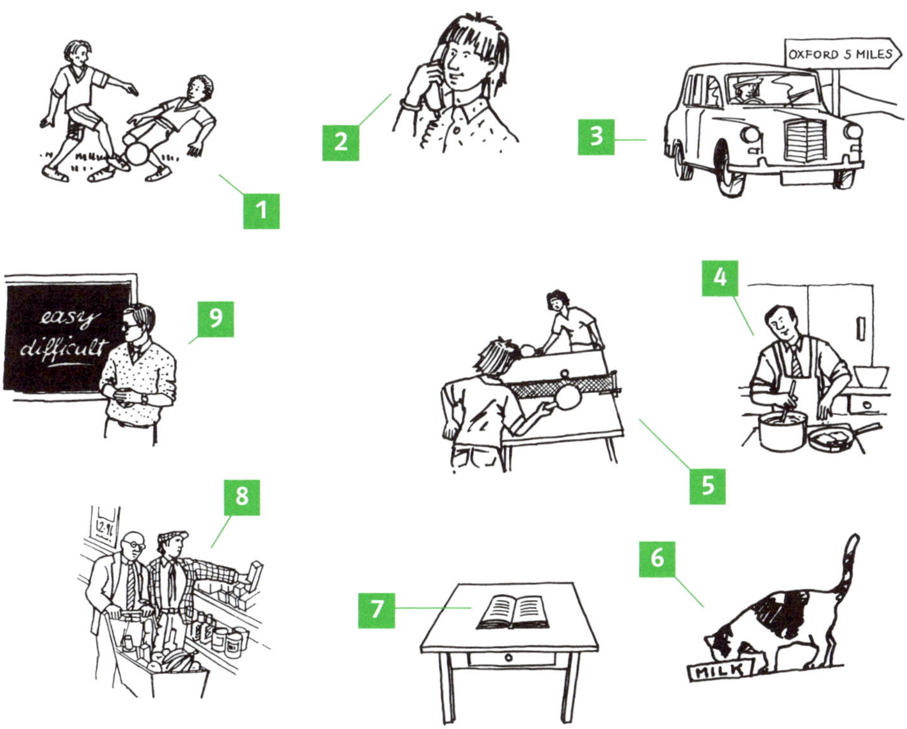

7

Jetzt sollst du zeigen, dass du die beiden Formen richtig anwenden kannst. Füge die (notwendigen) Satzteile zusammen, damit zwei richtige Sätze entstehen. Die Signalwörter helfen dir dabei.

1. Now Sometimes	Sylvia	is doing her homework. does her homework in the garden.

2. We	never	are smoking smoke	now. cigarettes.

3. Do you Are you	speaking speak	English	often? now?

4. He	doesn't isn't	sitting sit	there	every day. now.

5. They	cycle are cycling	to school	this week. every morning.

Wie bilde ich Fragen und Verneinungen?

Bei der Zeitform *simple present* brauchen wir bei Fragen und Verneinungen die entsprechenden Formen von *to do.*

Aussage	**Verneinung**	**Frage**
I live in Bristol.	I don't live in London.	Do you live here?
She lives near me.	She doesn't live there.	Where does he live?

Bei Sätzen mit Hilfsverben brauchen wir *to do* bei Fragen und Verneinungen nicht:

Aussage	**Verneinung**	**Frage**
I'm waiting for bus.	He's not waiting for the bus.	Is he waiting for the the bus?
I've got my ticket.	I haven't got my ticket.	Have you got yours?

Auch bei Sätzen mit *to be* als Vollverb wird *to do* in Fragen und Verneinungen nicht benötigt:

Aussage	**Verneinung**	**Frage**
He's here.	He isn't here.	Is he here?

8

Kannst du Fragen (?) bzw. Verneinungen (X) bilden?

Beispiel:

He speaks French.	(you ?)	→ Do you speak French?
We live in London.	(they X)	→ They don't live in London.
She likes ice-cream.	(What – you ?)	→ What do you like?

1.	They are English.	(X German)
2.	I live in Berlin.	(Where – you ?)
3.	We like ice-cream.	(they X)
4.	John reads comics.	(his sister Sheila X)
5.	Peter is writing a letter.	(Who … to ?)
6.	He often writes letters.	(X postcards)
7.	I've got a bike.	(she ?)
8.	We can speak German.	(X Welsh)
9.	My brother works in London.	(Where – your sister ?)
10.	These books cost £6.	(How much – those CDs ?)
11.	They are waiting for a bus.	(Which bus ?)
12.	He's upstairs in his room.	(What – do – there ?)

9

Hier musst du nicht nur die richtige Verbform (*simple present* oder *present progressive*), sondern auch ein zur Situation passendes Verb einsetzen.

1. "Hi, Paul. Is your sister Alex at home?" "No. She's in town.

   She ______________ some new shoes.

2. She always ______________ to town on Wednesday afternoons.

3. Can I ______________ her a message?"

4. "Yes. Would you and Alex to come to my party on Saturday?"

5. "Thanks, Jim. I'd love to come, and I'll ask Alex when she ___________ back.

6. Can we you at home this evening?"

7. "Well, we often ______________ swimming on Tuesday evenings."

8. "What time ______________ you usually ______________ back home after

   your swimming?" – "About eight." – "OK, I'll ring you after eight."

The present tense: simple and progressive forms

Simple	Progressive
Formen: I/we/you/they **live** here. He/she/it/Phil/Tania **lives** here.	**Formen:** I **am** stay**ing** here for a week. He/she/it/Phil/Tania **is** stay**ing** here for a week. We/you/they **are** learn**ing** French.
I/we/you/they **don't live** in London. He/she/it/Phil/Tania **doesn't live** in London.	**I'm/am not** learn**ing** Spanish. He/she/it/Phil/Tania **isn't** learn**ing** French. We/you/they **aren't** wait**ing** for anyone.
Do I/we/you/they **come** from London? **Does** he/she/Phil/Tania **come** from London?	**Am** I interrupt**ing** you? **Is** he/she/it disturb**ing** you? **Are** you/we/they wait**ing** for someone?
Verwendung: Gewohnheiten, Zustände, Tatsachen	**Verwendung:** Handlungen, die - im Augenblick des Sprechens ablaufen. - in einem länger andauernden gegenwärtigen Zeitraum ablaufen und als vorübergehend betrachtet werden.
Signalwörter: always, never, sometimes, often, usually, every week/month/day/year usw.	**Signalwörter:** now, at the moment, at present

Note 6!! Sabine hat überall Fehler gemacht!
Kannst du ihre Sätze korrigieren?

1. I learn English at the moment.

 ____

2. She are rarely going swimming.

 ____

3. My father is owning a big car now.

 ____

4. Lives John in Stuttgart?

 ____

5. My friend Peter is come to my house every week.

 ____

6. He do not know the answer.

 ____

7. Where do you going now?

 ____

8. I like not ice-cream.

 ____

9. On Mondays I am always arrived late at school.

10. Are liking you potatoes with your meat?

 ____

2 *Simple past* oder *past progressive*?

Wie im *present tense* gibt es auch im *past tense* eine einfache Form (z. B. *jumped*) und eine Verlaufsform (z. B. *were driving*). Da es im Deutschen diese Unterscheidung nicht gibt, werden bei der Verwendung von *simple past* und *past progressive* häufig Fehler gemacht.

Wann verwende ich *simple past*?

Bei Situationen in der Vergangenheit, in denen

1. eine Tatsache festgestellt wird:

   It **was** the first day of the summer holidays.
   Tania **didn't live** in the country.

2. eine Einzelhandlung von kurzer Dauer ausgedrückt wird:

   Tania **woke** early.

3. eine Reihe von aufeinander folgenden Handlungen in der Reihenfolge des Geschehens aufgelistet werden:

   Tania **jumped** out of bed, **ran** to the window, **pulled** back the curtains, **opened** the window and **looked** out across the garden.

Wann verwende ich *past progressive*?

Bei Situationen in der Vergangenheit, in denen eine oder mehrere Handlungen über längere Zeit stattfinden:

> The sun **was** already **shining** brightly through the window of her bedroom, and the birds **were singing**.

Beide Formen können miteinander kombiniert werden. Die Handlung in der Verlaufsform bildet den „Hintergrund" zu dem Ereignis im *simple past*.

> Tania suddenly **realized** that she **was** not **lying** in her own bed at home in London.

Diese Unterscheidung gibt es im Deutschen nicht. Deshalb ist es wichtig, die richtige Zeitform im Englischen zu wählen.

Verben, die nur kurze Handlungen ausdrücken und solche, die keine Handlungen, sondern Zustände, Besitzverhältnisse, Meinungen usw. ausdrücken, können nicht in der Verlaufsform verwendet werden.

Beispiele: to see, to hear, to break; to be, to become,
to like, to hate, to have, to owe, to own

While wird oft zusammen mit der Verlaufsform, *when* dagegen mit der einfachen Form benutzt.

While I **was waiting** for the bus, I **heard** an explosion.
I **was waiting** for the bus when I **heard** an explosion.

1

Beschreibe deinen Tag. Beginne ganz einfach. Bilde drei oder vier Sätze in einer Handlungskette:

"I got up at 7.45, washed, got dressed ..."

In einem zweiten Durchgang kannst du dann einige Hintergrundhandlungen in den Tagesverlauf einbauen:

"While I was walking to school I saw ..."

Hier solltest du mindestens fünf Sätze bilden können.

a) get up – have a shower – get dressed – have breakfast;
leave house – walk – arrive – talk to friends;
have English/PE/German – play in playground – write test;
go home – have lunch – do homework – watch TV/a video – listen to CD/music – go to bed

b) While I was ...-ing ... I saw/spoke to/listened to ...

2

Setze die in Klammern stehenden Verben in die jeweils richtige Form. In dieser Übung kommt jede Verbform in jedem Satz einmal vor.

Beispiel: (talk – ring) While we … to John the phone … .
While we were talking to John the phone rang.

1. (see – wait) I … an accident while I … for my train.
2. (get – fall) A young man … off the train when suddenly he … onto the platform.
3. (run – lie) Several people … over to help him because he … still … there when the train left.
4. (be – examine) A woman who said she … a doctor … him when my train arrived.
5. (leave – sit) I looked out of the window and just as my train … the young man … up.
6. (bake – go) I … a cake when the light … out.
7. (look – come) While I … for some candles the light … on again.
8. (have to – wait) I … finish the cake quickly because my friends … for it.
9. (be – give) It … a birthday cake, and one of my friends … a birthday party at his house.
10. (put – ring) I … the cake into a bag when the doorbell … .
11. (go – stand) I … to the door and opened it. Two of my friends … at the front door

3

Diese Übung ist etwas schwieriger. Es gibt nämlich keine Gewähr, dass jede Verbform einmal vorkommen muss. Je nach Zusammenhang kann zweimal die *simple form* oder die *progressive form* notwendig sein.

1. (be – arrive) It … a stormy night when Jenny … at Norwich Station.
2. (rain – blow) It … hard and a strong wind … .
3. (remember – not have) As she got off the train she … that she … an umbrella.
4. (go – phone) So she … into the station and … her friend Paul.
5. (get – ring) Paul … into the bath when the phone … .
6. (hear – get) As soon as he … the phone, Paul … out of the bath.
7. (take – wrap) He … a towel and … it round his waist.
8. (want – ring) Just as Paul … to pick up the phone, the doorbell … .
9. (drop – walk) He … the phone on a chair and … to the door of his flat.

10.	(go – hear)	He ... just ... into the hall when he ... the sound of water on the bathroom floor.
11.	(run – turn)	He ... into the bathroom and ... the water off.
12.	(open – stand)	Then he ... the front door. His friend Stan ... in the rain.
13.	(tell – come)	"Hi, Paul," said Stan. "Is Jenny here yet? She ... me she ... to visit you."
14.	(be – ring)	"Perhaps that ... her on the phone," said Paul. "I wanted to answer the phone when you ... the doorbell. Come in."
15.	(walk – pick)	He ... back into the living-room, but when he ... up the phone, there was no one there.
16.	(be)	Jenny ... already on her way to the flat in a taxi.

4

Was macht Tania auf dem Bauernhof ihres Onkels? Kannst du die Geschichte erzählen – natürlich unter Verwendung der richtigen Verben und Zeitformen? Jedes Verb darf nur einmal benutzt werden.

say, want, give, talk, see, answer, come, work, have, dring, arrive, sit

While Tania and her Uncle Jonathan ____________ breakfast, Jethro ____________ . Jethro ____________ on Uncle Jonathan's farm. Jethro ____________ down at the table and Uncle Jonathan ____________ him a cup of tea. Aunt Helen ____________ into the kitchen while they ____________ their tea. "Good morning, Jethro," she ____________ . "I ____________ you in the village yesterday. You ____________ to Joe Smith the policeman. What ____________ he ____________ to talk to you about?" "I'm afraid I can't tell you, Mrs Brown," Jethro ____________ "It's a secret."

while und *during*

Das wichtigste Signalwort für die *past progressive*-Form ist *while* (während).

While Tania was staying with her uncle and aunt, she met Jethro.

During heißt ebenfalls „während". Es wird aber nicht mit einem Verb, sondern mit einem Substantiv verwendet.

During her holiday/stay with her uncle and aunt, Tania met Jethro.

Weil es für beide englischen Wörter im Deutschen nur ein Wort gibt, kommt es oft zu Verwechslungen.

5

Setze das richtige Wort – *while* oder *during* – in die Sätze ein.

1. … my holidays I learnt to windsurf.
2. … Jean was having breakfast, the telephone rang.
3. I met Mr Jones … he was staying with our neighbours.
4. In Britain, they usually play football … the winter.
5. … we were playing basketball, the other pupils were doing a class test.
6. I read an interesting book … the flight to London.
7. … the first week of his stay in Britain he visited a lot of interesting places.
8. … my brother was asleep, I went into his room and borrowed his walkman.

6

Schreibe die Sätze um, indem du das jeweils andere Wort (*while* statt *during* und umgekehrt) einsetzt.

Beispiel: While I was staying at Brighton …
During my stay at Brighton …

1. While we were driving through the forest, we saw several bears.
2. During his walk in the park he got very wet.
3. I went to Bristol while I was staying in England last summer.
4. She phoned her boyfriend during her lunch break.
5. While we were performing "Hamlet", there was a fire in the school hall.
6. During our flight to New York the weather got worse.

7. The fans screamed all the time during the Rolling Stones' concert.
8. We stopped five times during our drive to Scotland.
9. While he was taking his exams, he lost about two kilos.

7

Schau dir die Bilder an und schreibe zu jedem Bild einen Satz, der meist – aber nicht immer – eine einfache und eine Verlaufsform enthalten wird.

while – play football – rain  1	when – have a bath – telephone ring  2	while – wait for the bus – read newspaper  3
when – girl wash hair – friend arrive  4	while – boys play cards – teacher enter  5	when – arrive at the hotel – sun set  6
while – watch TV – boy wash up  7	when – bus arrive – girl get on  8	while – postman deliver letters – dog attack/bite  9

The past tense: simple and progressive forms

Simple	Progressive
Formen: I/we/you/he/she/they **saw** him.	**Formen:** I/he/she **was** sitt**ing** in the garden. We/you/they **were** watch**ing** TV.
I/we/you/he/she/they **didn't talk** much.	I/he/she/it **wasn't** listen**ing**. We/you/they **weren't** wait**ing** for anyone.
Did I/we/he/she/it/you/they **see** the rainbow?	**Was** I/he/she/it wait**ing**? **Were** you/we/they listen**ing**?
Verwendung: Gewohnheiten, Zustände, Tatsachen, Einzelhandlungen und Handlungsketten in der Vergangenheit	**Verwendung:** Handlungen in der Vergangenheit von längerer Dauer
Signalwörter: yesterday, last week/month/year, when usw.	**Signalwörter:** while, during, at that time usw.

Meist bildet die Verlaufsform eine „Hintergrundhandlung“:

I **saw** my English teacher while I **was standing** at the bus stop.

Achtung:
Folgende Verben können nicht in der *progressive form* stehen
- Verben, die nur kurze Handlungen ausdrücken: *to see, to hear, to break* etc.
- Verben, die Zustände, Besitzverhältnisse, Meinungen usw. ausdrücken: *to be, to become, to like, to hate, to have, to own* etc.

Erinnerst du dich an Jethros Geheimnis (Übung 4)? Was war es? Du bekommst es heraus, wenn du die richtigen Ausdrücke in die Geschichte einsetzen kannst. Pass aber auf! Es sind mehr Wörter angegeben, als du brauchst, und du darfst jeden Ausdruck nur einmal benutzen.

while | during | were visiting | was seeing | when | were deciding | was ringing | watched | looked | saw | has been | ~~was~~ | visited | rang | decided | noticed

Sunday ___was___ Aunt Helen's birthday. On Saturday evenings, Aunt Helen and Uncle Jonathan usually __________ friends. Tania stayed at home that Saturday evening and watched TV. She was hungry, so she made herself a couple of sandwiches __________ one of the breaks. __________ she was watching a film, the doorbell __________ . She was alone in the farmhouse, so she __________ out of the window before she opened the door. Joe Smith the policeman was standing outside! When she __________ that Jethro and five or six other people were with him, she thought that something must be wrong! She opened the door. "Don't worry," said Jethro __________ he saw her anxious face. "This is our surprise for your Aunt Helen. Your aunt told me that she and your uncle __________ Mr and Mrs Jenkins down in the village tonight. So we __________ to have a little party with a few more friends. After all, they won't be back until nearly midnight – and your aunt's birthday starts then!"

3 *Simple past* oder *present perfect*?

3.1 Der Gebrauch des *simple past*

Wann verwende ich das *simple past*?

Das *simple past* ist immer die richtige Form, wenn der Satz eine Zeitangabe in der abgeschlossenen Vergangenheit enthält.

Wichtige Signalwörter:
yesterday, last Monday, last night, in 1994, two minutes ago, in December usw.

Zeitbestimmungen wie:
when I was young; as soon as she arrived;
when we lived in Birmingham

I **saw** Tina at school yesterday. (einmalige Kurzhandlung)
She **got** up, **washed, had** breakfast … (Handlungsfolge)
We **lived** in London for ten years when I was a boy. (längerer Zustand)

1

Setze die richtigen *simple past*-Formen in die Sätze ein. Wenn du Probleme hast, schlage einfach in einer Liste der unregelmäßigen Verben nach.

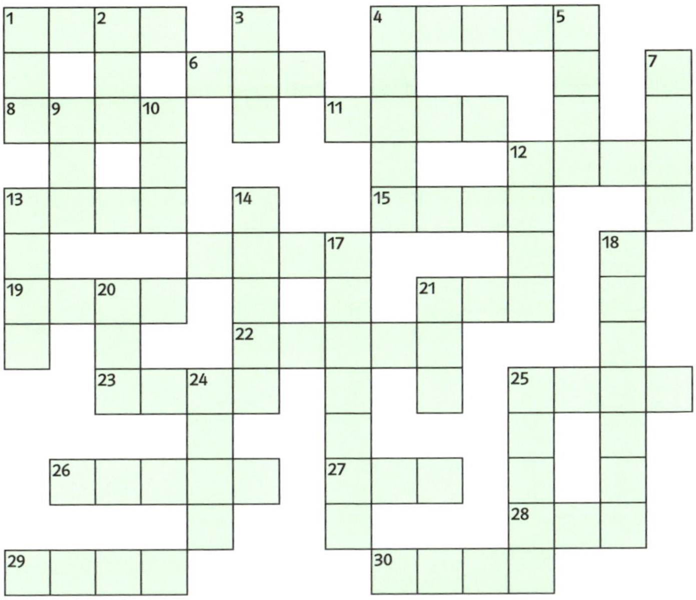

Across:

1. We … late for school.
4. He said "Hello" and I … his hand.
6. Her dog … me in the leg.
8. The choir … a folk song.
11. She slipped on a banana skin and … heavily.
12. We … across the river.
13. They … to bed at midnight.
15. She … her jeans on a sharp nail.
16. The hunters … the fox.
19. The sun … at 5.40 a.m.
21. He … at the table reading a book.
22. The car-thief … a brand-new Jaguar.
23. Tania … early that morning.
25. He walked out and … the door behind him.
26. Mr Smith cleaned the kitchen table and … the floor.
27. The dog … the bone in a hole in the ground.
28. She … on her best clothes and went to the party.
29. After six whiskies he … ill.
30. I … my passport last week. I couldn't find it anywhere.

Down:

1. What … his name?
2. The boys … home quickly.
3. She … the fire at 6.30 p.m.
4. He … his name "Greene" with an "e" at the end.
5. The teacher … the answers to our questions.
7. He knocked at the door and … into the room.
9. He never … fish and chips.
10. They … married last year.
12. I … her a ticket for the concert last week.
13. She never … dresses – always jeans and T-shirts.
14. We had a choice of colours, so we … a green one.
17. I … about getting a job, but I finally decided to stay at school.
18. She … me some flowers from her garden.
20. They … the film last month.
21. His mother took out some plates and … the table for tea.
24. Our teacher … our exercise books for over a week. He said he had been too busy to mark our homework!
25. I was so tired that I … until midday.

2

Ergänze mit der Vergangenheitsform des Verbs aus dem ersten Satzteil.

Beispiel: Sally White lives in London now, but when she was a girl she lived in Bristol.

1. Usually Sally gets up early, but yesterday morning she ___________ up late.
2. She sometimes takes an hour to get ready for work, but yesterday she only ___________ twenty minutes.
3. She seldom goes to work by car, and yesterday she ___________ to work by bus, as usual.
4. Normally Sally does not run to the bus stop, but on that day she ___________ as fast as she could.
5. There are always a lot of people on the bus to work, but this morning there ___________ only about ten.
6. The bus-driver usually drives quite fast, but yesterday he ___________ slowly.
7. Sally often sees friends on the bus, but on that day she ___________ no one she knew.
8. Sometimes people speak to her on the bus. Yesterday nobody ___________ to her.
9. "I don't know what's wrong with everybody this morning," she thought. But when she arrived at work she ___________ she had made a mistake.
10. The bank where Sally works stands on the corner of a street. Sally ___________ in front of the locked door for a minute or two before she realized what was wrong. Yesterday was Sunday.

3

a) Schreibe die *present perfect*-und *simple past*-Formen in zwei Spalten auf. Prüfe die Richtigkeit deiner Lösungen, bevor du weitermachst.

Joe: "Did you see Andy Wilson at the pub last night?"
Jethro: "No, I haven't seen him for days. Was he at the pub last night?"
Joe: "He hasn't been at the pub since last Saturday. He's been away all week."
Jethro: "What did you want to see him about, Joe?"
Joe: "Someone stole three or four sheep from Farmer Hunt's field one night last week."
Jethro: "What makes you think that Andy stole them?"
Joe: "Well, he's the only person in the village who has suddenly disappeared."
Jethro: "But I've known Andy for thirty years! He's never stolen anything!"
Joe: "Well, we found two of the sheep in his barn yesterday."
Jethro: "That doesn't mean he stole them! Have you phoned his sister in London yet?"
Joe: "I didn't know he had a sister in London."
Jethro: "Maybe he's gone to visit her. He was always talking about going to London. I'll ring her tonight. And I wouldn't talk to anyone about sheep-stealing if I were you, Joe. Let's keep it a secret until we can find out more."

b) Hast du alles verstanden? Das wollen wir gleich prüfen. Setze die Satzteile richtig zusammen.

	has never stolen	some sheep last week
	hasn't been to the pub	about Andy's sister.
Andy Wilson	wasn't at the pub	since Saturday.
Jethro	hasn't seen Andy	last night.
Joe Smith	has known	for some days.
Someone	didn't know	Andy for years.
	hasn't phoned	Andy's sister yet.
	stole	anything in his life.

3.2 Der Gebrauch des *present perfect*

Wann verwende ich das *present perfect*?

Das *present perfect* ist auf jeden Fall richtig,

1. wenn der Satz keine Zeitangabe in der Vergangenheit enthält. Hier ist die Tatsache, nicht der Zeitpunkt wichtig. Vergleiche:

Present perfect – Tatsache wichtig	**Simple past** – Zeitpunkt/-spanne wichtig
A: **Have** you **seen** Andy? B: No, I **haven't**. A: **Have** you **done** your homework? B: Yes, I **have**.	A: **Didn't** you **see** him yesterday? B: No, I **didn't**. A: When **did** you **do** it? B: I **did** it before I came home.

Eine vergangenheitsbezogene Frage mit *when*? wird immer im *simple past* gestellt, weil ja eine Zeitangabe erfragt wird.

"**When did** you do your homework?"

2. wenn eine ausgedehnte Handlung zwar in der Vergangenheit anfängt, aber bis in die Gegenwart hinein dauert. Vergleiche:

I **have lived** here for 10 years. (Ich lebe hier seit 10 Jahren.)	I **lived** here for 10 years. (Ich wohnte mal 10 Jahre lang hier.)

Im ersten Satz weiß man, dass die Person immer noch (und vermutlich bis auf weiteres) dort wohnt, während sie im zweiten Satz auf jeden Fall nicht mehr dort wohnt, sondern mal dort gewohnt hat.

3. wenn eine Handlung in der Gegenwart zu Ende geht. Dieser Bezug zur Gegenwart gibt der Zeitform auch ihren Namen ***present** perfect*.

Present perfect	**Simple past**
– Vollendung in der Gegenwart She **has** just **finished** the book. They **have arrived** at last! **Signalwörter:** just, at last, now, since, not … yet, ever? *(in Fragen)*	– Vollendung in der Vergangenheit She finished the book last week. They arrived late last time, too. **Signalwörter:** last week, yesterday, etc.

4

Zunächst einmal eine leichte Übung. Wähle das passende Verb und setze es in der richtigen Form des *present perfect* ein. Jedes Verb darf nur einmal benutzt werden.

look write see promise fly go be get arrive have

a) In the school playground at 8.45 a.m.

1. "_______ you ____________________ John this morning?"
2. "No,but I _______ just ____________________."
3. Perhaps he _______ already ____________________ to his classroom."
4. "No. I _______ already ____________________ in his classroom. There's nobody there."

b) At the youth club one Friday evening.

5. "How's your sister Stella? She _______n't ____________________ to the youth club for a few weeks."
6. "Didn't you know? She _______ to the USA for a year.
7. She _______ a job as an au-pair girl."
8. "Lucky Stella! _______ she ____________________ a letter home yet?"
9. "No, she _______n't ____________________ time. She only left yesterday.
10. But she ____________________ to phone as soon as she can."

just

Die Bedeutung des englischen Wortes *just* hängt davon ab, mit welcher Zeitform es benutzt wird. Mit der *progressive form* oder mit dem *present perfect* heißt es „gerade", „soeben":

We were just waiting for the bus when John arrived.
You're not late. The others have only just arrived.

Mit dem *simple present* oder *simple past* heißt es „einfach", „nur":

I just want to know where he lives. Ich will nur wissen …
She just stared at me. Sie starrte mich einfach an.

5

Bilde Sätze, in denen das Wort *just* die richtige Bedeutung erhält.

We have just	hope you know what you're doing!
I just	shouted at me. He wouldn't listen.
She has just	gone. If you run, you'll catch her up.
He just	didn't listen to their friends' advice.
They have just	thought you might want to come with us.
We just	seen a ghost.
I have just	sold their house.
They just	received a letter from Stella.

6

Setze das vorgegebene Verb in der richtigen Zeitform ein.

1. **(do)**	"What … you … last night?"
2. **(watch)**	"I … TV until midnight.
3. **(be)**	There … a good programme on BBC2 about whales."
4. **(see)**	"I … many good programmes on BBC2 recently."
5. **(watch)**	"… you … the same programme?"
6. **(not have)**	"I … time to watch TV last night.
7. **(be)**	We … very busy lately.
8. **(see)**	But we … a film about Wales last Friday. Perhaps it was the same film.
9. **(show)**	It … all the tourist attractions.
10. **(see)**	"… you ever … whales?"
11. **(go)**	"Wales? We … there last year.
12. **(misunderstand)**	"But you … me.
13. **(not mean/mean)**	I … Wales – I … whales: w – h – a – l – e – s !"
14. **(see)**	"Oh! Yes, we … several whales during our summer holidays.
15. **(see)**	… you ever … a whale in the sea?" "No, only on TV."

7

Der Polizist Joe Smith möchte einige Fragen an Andy Wilson stellen, der inzwischen von seinem Besuch in London zurückgekehrt ist. Joe möchte die Fragen vorher aufschreiben, damit er nichts vergisst. Kannst du ihm dabei helfen?

Beispiel: Last Friday night – Where?
Where were you last Friday night?

1. Ever keep sheep in your barn *(Scheune)?*
2. See sheep in Farmer Hunt's field last week?
3. Ever be to London?
4. First visit to London – When?
5. Stay with sister?
6. Sister in London – How long?
7. Back to your farm – When?
8. Find sheep in barn?
9. Phone police?
10. Why not?

Ob es Andy gewesen ist? Was glaubst du?

8

Hier bist du als Journalist gefragt. Kannst du die Informationen über den berühmten Popsänger Johnny Purple für einen Zeitschriftenartikel in komplette Sätze umformulieren? In der richtigen Zeitform, versteht sich.

★ Born 1980
★ 1980 – 1997: London
★ 1986 – 1996: Croydon Comprehensive School
★ 1996 – 1997: work as assistant in music shop; guitar lessons for two years
★ 1998 – now: singer in pop group "Johnny's Purple Hearts"
★ Six singles and one CD so far
★ Three tours in Europe and America
★ Tour to South Africa last year
★ Married Sally Johnson in 2004
★ Divorce one year later

Simple past oder *present perfect?*

Ganz wichtig für die Wahl des *simple past* ist das Vorhandensein eines abgeschlossenen Zeitraums in der Vergangenheit.

Am Nachmittag fragt man:

"**Did** you **see** John this morning?"

Der Vormittag („this morning") gilt hier als **abgeschlossener Zeitraum**.

Ist der Vormittag noch nicht vorbei, muss dieselbe Frage so lauten:

"**Have** you **seen** John this morning?"

Ein weiteres Beispiel:
"I **have been** to London."
"I **was** in London last week."

Beide Sätze können sich auf denselben Besuch beziehen. Der Unterschied liegt darin, dass im ersten Satz nur eine Feststellung (ohne Zeitangabe) gemacht wird, während im zweiten Satz der abgeschlossene Zeitraum angegeben wird.

Setze die richtige Zeitform des in Klammern stehenden Verbs in folgende Sätze ein. Klammern im Satz bedeuten, dass möglicherweise – aber nicht unbedingt – ein Hilfsverb zur Zeitenbildung benötigt wird:

1. (do) "_________ you _________ your homework yet?"
2. (do) "Yes, Mum. I _________ it when I got home from school."
3. (tell) "That's what you _________ me yesterday!"
4. (believe) "It was true! You just _________n't _______________ me!"
5. (finish) "Are you sure you __________________ everything before you put the TV on?"
6. (come) "Yes, Mum. _________ Dad _________ home from work?"
7. (arrive) "Yes. He (_________) just __________________. Why?"
8. (say) "Well, a few days ago he _________ he would test my French vocabulary with me.
9. (have) We _________n't _________ a French vocabulary test for about a month, but we've got one tomorrow."
10. (have) "_________n't your class _________ a vocabulary test on Monday?"
"Yes, Mum. But that was for German. French is tomorrow."

4 *Simple present perfect* oder *present perfect progressive?*

4.1 *Simple present perfect* und *present perfect progressive* im Vergleich

Wann benötige ich die Verlaufsform des *present perfect*?

simple present perfect ⟷	**present perfect progressive**
I **have read** the book. You can have it back.	I **have been reading** all afternoon.
= Fertige Handlung, die zu einem unwichtigen Zeitpunkt in der Vergangenheit zu Ende ging.	= Beschreibung eines Verlaufs, der bis in die Gegenwart hineinragt und auch fortgesetzt werden kann – keine abgeschlossene Handlung
= *present perfect* ***simple***	= *present perfect* ***progressive***

Das Unterscheidungsmerkmal zwischen einfacher und Verlaufsform ist „Tatsache" ↔ „Beschreibung".

He **lived** here all his life.	Tatsache – jetzt ist er aber tot
I **have lived** here all my life.	Tatsache – „Handlung" geht weiter
I **have been living** here **for** three weeks/**since** August 1st.	Beschreibung einer ausgedehnten Handlung, besonders mit *for/since*

Bei Verben wie z. B. *live, work, learn, wait, play, watch, listen* usw. sowie mit *for/since* wird meist die Verlaufsform verwendet.

1

Hier eine leichte Übung nur mit dem *present perfect progressive*. Jedes Verb darf nur einmal benutzt werden.

live stand do eat learn lie wait play listen drink watch work

1. "How long … you … English?" – "For two years."
2 My cousin … here since 1986
3. We … n't … here long – only about ten minutes.
4. "Since when … your brother … at the supermarket?" – "Since last month."
5. " … Julie … tennis all afternoon?" – "Yes – since lunchtime."
6. Radio announcer: "You … to a live pop concert from the Royal Albert Hall in London."
7. "Have you seen my English vocab notebook?" – "Yes. It … on the table in the hall all week."
8. "What … you … all evening?" –
9. "We … an interesting programme about Britain on TV."
10. "How long … we … for the bus?" – "About an hour."
11. The children aren't hungry. They … crisps all evening.
12. "Someone … my juice! The carton is nearly empty!"

2

Jetzt geht's um die richtige Form – *simple* oder *progressive*?

1. **(do – work)**	"What … you … all afternoon?" – "I … in the garden."
2. **(do – finish)**	"... you … your homework yet?" – "Yes, I … just … ."
3. **(write – not post)**	"... you … to your uncle?" – "Yes, but I .... the letter yet."
4. **(use – not see)**	"Who … my pen? I can't find it." – "I … it anywhere."
5. **(be – look)**	"Where … you ...? I … for you all morning!"
6. **(go – do)**	"All the lights … just … out. What … you ...?" –
7. **(not do – sit)**	"I … anything. John and I … in the kitchen all evening."
8. **(eat – eat)**	"You've got chocolate around your mouth. … you … my chocolates again?" – "Me? No – I … anything since lunch."
9. **(stand – watch)**	"Look at these cigarette ends on the ground under the window! Someone … here for a long time in the dark and … us through the window!"
10. **(stand – think)**	"I … often … here waiting for a bus." – "... you ever … of taking a taxi?"

4.2 *for* und *since*

Wie verwende ich *for* und *since*?

since

We **have lived** here **since** 1992 (and we are still living here).

since = seit + Ausgangszeitpunkt: 1992 = bis heute – und bis auf weiteres

for

We **have lived** here **for** three years.

for = seit + Zeitspanne: X Tage/Monate/Jahre bis heute – und bis auf weiteres

Vergleiche die deutsche Ausdrucksweise mit der einfachen Gegenwart:

„Wir **leben** hier **seit** 1992."

for kann auch für abgeschlossene Zeiträume in der Vergangenheit benutzt werden. Dann steht es mit dem *simple past.*

He **lived** here **for** three years. (Er wohnte hier drei Jahre **lang**.)

Bei „seit" = *for/since* heißt es eben: Gut aufpassen! Und auf keinen Fall *for* mit dem deutschen „vor" verwechseln!

Er wohnte hier **vor** drei Jahren. (He lived here three years **ago**.)

3

Schau dir das Diagramm an und vergleiche die Angaben mit den Aussagen der fünf Personen. Wer sagt was?

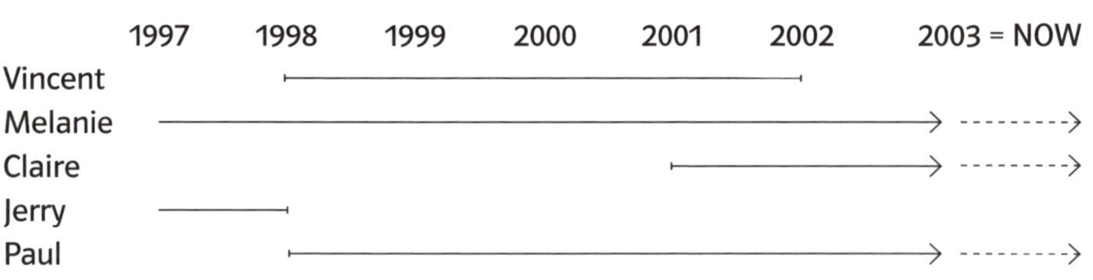

1. "I have lived in London for six years."
2. "I lived in London for four years."
3. "I lived in London five years ago."
4. "I have lived in London since 1998."
5. "I have lived in London since two years ago."

4

Die englische Abkürzung *„CV"* heißt *„curriculum vitae"* (Lebenslauf). Wenn du eine Stelle suchst, musst du in der Regel einen Lebenslauf einreichen. In Vincents Lebenslauf aber fehlen die Wörter *for, since* und *ago*. Setze sie richtig ein!

I was born in London 16 years ____________ but I have lived in Birmingham ____________ my parents moved there in 1986. My father worked as a clerk ____________ 15 years but he had to give up his office job five years ____________ and has been a postman ____________ 2001. My mother has worked in a kindergarten ____________ I started grammar school five years ____________. I have one brother aged 18 and a younger sister aged 12. I am looking for a job now. ____________ May I have written to several firms. I wrote to your firm some weeks ____________ but have not received any answer yet, so I am writing again. Please let me know if you have any holiday jobs left.

5

Wie wär's mit einem *Wordsearch-Puzzle*? Die Verbformen zur Ergänzung der folgenden Sätze findest du im „Buchstabensalat" (ein Partizip haben wir für dich umkringelt). Die anderen liegen waagerecht, senkrecht oder quer (von oben links nach unten rechts) im ganzen Block verteilt.

A	L	O	S	T	Z	B	F	B	S
S	W	P	P	Q	S	E	E	N	P
K	U	W	O	N	A	G	A	E	E
G	T	A	K	E	N	U	T	R	N
N	I	K	E	T	D	N	E	T	T
G	O	V	N	W	G	O	N	E	N
D	R	I	E	E	N	N	N	S	Y
G	A	S	P	N	N	T	S	E	M

1. John has … his English book. – 2. Have you … to your teacher yet? – 3. Who has … my umbrella? – 4. My friends have … the film twice already. – 5. Who has … all the bananas? – 6. They have all … to the open-air concert. – 7. Where have you … ? I've been looking for you everywhere! – 8. Be quiet when you go into the cinema, please. The film has already … . 9. Have you … your homework yet? – 10. They have never … a prize in the lottery yet. – 11. I've just … my mother some flowers. It's her birthday. – 12. They have … all their money.

Present perfect: simple and progressive forms

Simple	Progressive
Formen: I/we/you/they **have seen** her. He/she/Phil/Tania **has seen** the new film. I/we/you/they **haven't been** there. He/she/it/Phil/Tania **hasn't been** there. **Have** I/we/you/they ever **been** there? **Has** he/she/Phil/Tania ever **been** there?	**Formen:** I/you/we/they **have been** wait**ing** for ages. He/she/it/Phil/Tania **has been** wait**ing** for ages. I/we/you/they **haven't been** wait**ing** long. He/she/it/Phil/Tania **hasn't been** wait**ing** long. **Have** I/we/you/they **been** wait**ing** long? **Has** he/she/it/Tania **been** wait**ing** long?
Verwendung: 1. Einzelhandlungen in der Vergangenheit ohne Zeitangabe; 2. Öfter wiederholte Handlungen, die in der Vergangenheit und bis heute wiederholt wurden; 3. Einzelhandlungen, die in der Vergangenheit anfangen und bis in die Gegenwart andauern.	**Verwendung:** Bei Handlungen und Zuständen von längerer Dauer, die sich meist bis in die Gegenwart und vermutlich auch darüber hinaus erstrecken.
Signalwörter: always, never, sometimes, often, since, for	**Signalwörter:** for, since

Setze die richtigen Ausdrücke aus dem Kasten in die Sätze ein. Achtung: Der Kasten enthält mehr Wörter, als du brauchst, und du darfst jeden Ausdruck nur einmal benutzen.

for	since	have deserved	waited	have been walking		
been	have been arriving	walked	have been deserving			
have been waiting	have	arrived	have been sending			
send	did	didn't	arrive	sent	has	hasn't

Late for the disco

"Where ___________ you ___________? I ___________________________ for you ___________ half an hour!"

"Sorry I'm late. I ______________________ over twenty minutes for a bus. But in the end I ______________________ here. Let me sit down. I'm so tired! I feel as if I _____________________________________ all afternoon!"

"Never mind. Sit down. If you walked all the way you ____________________ a rest!"

"Where's Geoff? _____________ he _________________ yet?"

"He _____________ just _____________ me an SMS. He's standing outside the wrong disco! He's been there _____________ seven o'clock. I sent him an SMS back. He'll be here in a few minutes."

5 Das *past perfect*

Englisch:
After he **had finished** his computer game, he **went** to bed.

Deutsch:
Nachdem er sein Computerspiel **beendet hatte**, **ging** er ins Bett.

Eigentlich wird die Vorvergangenheit – das *past perfect* – im Englischen genauso verwendet wie im Deutschen. Wenn da nicht wieder die verflixte *progressive form* wäre … Zum Glück gelten viele Regeln für die Verwendung der Verlaufsform auch für diese Zeitstufe.

5.1 Der Gebrauch des *simple past perfect*

Die Zeitform **past perfect** (Vorvergangenheit) zeigt an, dass eine Handlung **vor einer anderen Handlung abgeschlossen** (= „perfekt") war.

Vergleiche: I ate my breakfast in bed and then got up.
1 2

I ate my breakfast after I had got up.
2 1

Beim zweiten Satz zeigt die Zeitform *(past perfect)* an, welche der beiden Handlungen vor der anderen passierte, und zwar ganz unabhängig von der Reihenfolge im Satz. Die Vorvergangenheit wird meist im selben Satz mit einer Handlung in der einfachen Vergangenheit (niemals im *present perfect*!) kontrastiert.

In der Reihenfolge der Handlungen kann es keine Verwechslung geben. Die *past perfect*-Form wird immer für Handlung 1 verwendet. Oft reicht zur Kontrastierung auch ein Vergangenheitsbezug (ohne eine *simple past*-Form im Satz):

He had never been there before. – Er war nie vorher dort gewesen.

Die wichtigsten Signalwörter:

1. After — **After** they **had gone**, we did the washing up.
She phoned her boyfriend **after** she **had finished** her homework.

2.	Before	Besonders wenn die erste Handlung nur „theoretisch" war bzw. durch die zweite unterbrochen wurde: **Before** I **had started** breakfast the doorbell rang. They arrived **before** I **had finished**.
3.	Because	Begründungen mit because stehen oft im *past perfect* : I moved away from Birmingham **because I had never liked** the place.

1

Lies den folgenden Text durch und schreibe (in verkürzter Form) die Sätze auf, die *past perfect* -Formen enthalten.

The computer exhibition

Last week some friends and I wanted to go to the National Computer Exhibition in Birmingham. My boyfriend Geoff had read about it in a magazine and because we all had a Young Person's Railcard, we decided to take the train. We arrived at the station early, bought our tickets, went to platform 1, got on the train that was standing there, and waited for it to start. After we had waited for about a quarter of an hour, Peter got out again and asked a porter if it was the right train to Birmingham Exhibition Centre.
The porter laughed and told us that the train to Birmingham had left ten minutes ago. The train we were sitting in was not leaving until an hour later. Geoff told the porter that the man at the ticket office had said "Platform 1", and the porter said the man had meant "the front end of Platform 1". We had got into the last coach. The train to Birmingham had been the first four coaches at the front end of the platform. They had already gone, and we had been in one of the last four coaches which had been left behind.
So we went and had a cup of coffee and waited for the next train to Birmingham Exhibition Centre.

Prüfe deine Lösung im Schlüssel, bevor du weitermachst. Hast du dir auch die eine Passivform im *past perfect* aufgeschrieben?

2

Jetzt zur Abwechslung eine kleine Bildgeschichte zum Thema Zelten. Zu jedem Bild schreibst du einen Satz, der die vorhergehende Handlung nochmals aufgreift.

Beispiel:
Jean and Sheila decided to go camping. → After they had decided to go camping, they checked their camping equipment.

Dein erster Satz fängt also mit *„After they had checked their …"* an. Das Verb für die nächste Handlung steht über jedem Bild.

pack

cycle

find

go shopping

make and eat supper

go to bed

3

Aus zwei mach eins: Verbinde die beiden Sätze mit *after* oder *because*. Vergiss nicht, dass die Reihenfolge der Handlungen nicht immer der Reihenfolge der Sätze entspricht. Bei Sätzen mit (x) dahinter gibt es 2 oder manchmal sogar 3 Lösungsmöglichkeiten. Schreibe sie alle auf.

1. We bought tickets. We went to the pop concert. (x)
2. They sold their house. They bought a bungalow. (x)
3. I phoned the police. My car was stolen.
4. She left school. She found a job. (x)
5. Did you go to Brighton? You visited London.
6. I phoned the number quickly and got the job.
7. The woman shouted at the girl. She burned the cakes.

8. We found out their address. We wrote them a letter.
9. He phoned his parents. He arrived in England
10. I passed my driving test. I bought a motor-bike. (x)
11. I went to the lost-property office. I lost my umbrella. (x)
12. They lost the rugby match. They drank a lot of beer. (x)
13. We came to London. We wanted to improve our English.
14. She went swimming. She bought a new bikini. (x)
15. The tourists visited the castle. They went back to their hotel.

4

Jetzt sollst du die Sätze eigenständig zu Ende führen. Vervollständige die Sätze mit Hilfe der in Klammern stehenden Wörter. (Dies ist die Fortsetzung der Geschichte über die Computerausstellung).

Beispiele:
We (take) the next train to Birmingham after (drink – cup of coffee).

We took the next train to Birmingham after we had drunk a cup of coffee.

The train (stop) before we (arrive – station).

The train stopped before we had arrived at the station.

1. We (look) at the scenery after the train (leave – station).
2. After we (pass Rugby Station) the train (go) into a long tunnel.
3. Suddenly the train (stop) before we (reach – end – tunnel).
4. After the train (stop) the guard (come) into our coach.
5. He (want) to know if anyone (pull – emergency brake = Notbremse).
6. Nobody (said) anything because nobody (pull – brake).
7. Some passengers (be) frightened because (train – stop – tunnel).
8. After (guard – tell – passengers) that there was no need to worry, he (speak – driver – train telephone).
9. Before (guard – finish speaking) we (hear) the driver's voice over the coach loudspeakers.
10. He (tell) us that there (be) a small fault in the train's computer system but that everything (be) OK now.
11. Five minutes later the train (start to move again).

5.2 Der Gebrauch des *past perfect progressive*

Die Verlaufsform der Vorvergangenheit betont eine länger andauernde Handlung. Sie wird, wie alle Verlaufsformen, mit der *ing*-Form gebildet.

Vergleiche:

We went down to the beach after we **had had** breakfast.
We reached the beach after we **had been walking** for about ten minutes.

Da die Verlaufsform einen „Verlauf" ausdrückt, wird sie nicht bei Tätigkeiten verwendet, die von kurzer Dauer sind.

Vergleiche:

After we **had moved** to London, we lost contact with our friends in Leeds. (Der Umzug dauerte nicht lange.)
After we **had been living** in London for a while, we lost contact with our friends in Leeds.

Verben, die oft in der Verlaufsform stehen, sind z.B.:
to live, to work, to study, to learn, to watch **(aber nicht *to see*),**
to listen **(aber nicht *to hear*),** to stay, to travel, to talk

Verben, die Zustände (to be, to become) oder sehr kurze Handlungen beschreiben, können nicht in der Verlaufsform benutzt werden z.B.:

to start, to stop, to finish, to see, to hear,
to arrive, to take, to be, to become

5

Zuerst eine etwas leichtere Übung. In jedem Satz wird die *past perfect progressive*-Form des Verbs benutzt.

1. (live) "How long ... you ... here before you moved to London?" – "Three years."
2. (study) He started to learn French after he ... English for two years.
3. (drink) People ... 'Wonder-Cola' for years before scientists discovered that it was a serious danger to health.
4. (wait) The bus only arrived after the passengers ... in the rain for almost an hour.

5. **(work)** She became the boss's assistant before she ... at the firm for six months.
6. **(do)** "You looked very dirty when I saw you yesterday! What ... you ... ?"
7. **(dig)** "I ... the garden."
8. **(not play)** The pop group ... long when the fire started.
9. **(smoke)** "How long ... she ... cigarettes before her doctor told her to stop?" – "Only about two years."

6

Hier ist mal die einfache Form, mal die Verlaufsform des *past perfect* gefragt.

Prüfe die Lösungen der ersten vier Sätze, bevor du mit den restlichen weitermachst, denn hier musst du dir die Verben selbst einfallen lassen!

1. **(write)** In an interview last week, the pop star Johnny Purple said that he ... songs for many years but that he (not write) ... a really successful one since 1994
2. **(collect)** My friend told me that he ... CDs since 1989 and that he ... now ... over 300
3. **(travel)** He ... never ... by Underground before. After he ... for a quarter of an hour he realized he was going in the wrong direction.
4. **(drive)** "How long ... you ... before you had your first accident?" – "Three years – but I ... over 100,000 kilometres in that time, so it wasn't surprising!"

FOOTBALL IN THE PARK

5. We ... football in the park for half an hour when a park keeper came up and told us to stop. We told him we ... always ... football there.
6. The man said he ... as a park keeper for 25 years and that football had never been allowed in the park.
7. We just laughed. None of us knew him – none of us ... ever ... him before. He began to get angry and warned us that he would be back in five minutes. Then he began to walk away.
8. Just then an old man who ... us play came over and began to speak to the park keeper.
9. After they ... for about a minute the old man came over and spoke to us. "You can carry on playing," he said. "What about the park keeper?" I asked. "Don't worry about him!" said the old man. "He won't be back! When I was a keeper in this park 30 years ago, he and his friends played football here every day!"

The past perfect: simple and progressive forms

Formen:
Wie beim *present perfect* wird zur Bildung des *past perfect* immer eine Form von *to have* gebraucht.

After I **had seen** the film …	Nachdem ich den Film gesehen hatte …
After we **had gone** …	Nachdem wir weggegangen waren …
After we **had been waiting** …	Nachdem wir gewartet hatten …

Signalwörter: after, before

Wichtigstes Signalwort für das *past perfect* ist *after*. *Before* wird mit dem *past perfect* oft bei Handlungen benutzt, die nicht geschehen konnten oder noch nicht beendet waren, als sie unterbrochen wurden.

Before I had finished speaking, the people began to shout at me.

Kombinationen:

1. sehr häufig als Kontrast zu einer späteren Handlung im selben Satz, die dann im *simple past* steht.

2. seltener allein im Satz, aber auch dann nur zusammen mit Sätzen, die im *simple past* stehen.

   John arrived late. The food **had been eaten** and the wine **had been drunk**. His friends **had** all **gone** home. Only a few strangers were standing around.

Indirekte Rede:
Das *past perfect* ist ziemlich oft in der indirekten Rede anzutreffen. Alle Verben, die in der direkten Rede im *simple past, present perfect* oder *past perfect* gesprochen werden, werden nach einem Einführungsverb in der Vergangenheit (*he told me, she said…* usw.) um eine Zeitstufe „nach hinten" verschoben und stehen dann in der *past perfect*-Form (siehe Kap. 12.2).

He told me that he **had had** an accident on the way to school. She said that she **had finished** her homework.

Schon wieder Note 6!! Diesmal ist es Timo, der alles falsch hat! Kannst du ihm helfen, die richtigen Zeitformen einzusetzen?

1. After I have finished my homework, I watched TV.

   ____

2. I had learnt English for two years before I had gone to Britain for the first time.

   ____

3. She finished her lunch long before I had arrived.

   ____

4. My father had driven for half an hour when he realized that he was on the wrong road.

   ____

5. He told me that he borrowed my book.

   ____

6. After he went home I saw that he forgot to take his CDs with him.

   ____

7. When he arrived I told him that he had been late.

   ____

8. I have gone out to play football with them after I had finished my homework.

   ____

9. Before I had been getting up I already had breakfast – in bed!

   ____

10. We had been walking to the station before the rain began, so we didn't get wet.

    ____

6 *Will-future, going to-future* und *present progressive*

Im Deutschen spielt das Futur eine geringe Rolle. In der gesprochenen Sprache wird es häufig durch das Präsens ersetzt: „Ich fliege nächste Woche nach Spanien“ ist geläufiger als „Ich werde nächste Woche nach Spanien fliegen“. Ganz anders im Englischen! Hier werden zukünftige Handlungen mit Verbformen wiedergegeben, die Zukunft ausdrücken. Und zwar nicht nur mit einer bestimmten Verbform, sondern mit mehreren – je nachdem, ob es sich um eine reine Absichtserklärung, eine Vermutung oder eine feste Vereinbarung handelt.

Wie drücke ich eine Handlung in der Zukunft aus?

1. Hast du eine zukünftige Zeitangabe im Satz (z. B. *tonight, tomorrow, next week, on Monday, next month*) dann solltest du das ***present progressive*** benutzen:

   "Can you come to my party next week?"
   "I'm sorry. We**'re flying** to Spain for a week next Monday."
   („Wir fliegen nächsten Montag nach Spanien.“)

   Wie immer bei der Verlaufsform gilt auch hier: *present progressive* ist nur bei Verben möglich, die einen Verlauf ausdrücken (vgl. Kap. 5.2)

2. Handelt es sich um etwas, was man in der Zukunft zu tun beabsichtigt, ohne zu wissen, ob alles wirklich so abläuft, wie man sich das vorstellt, dann verwendest du am besten ***going to* mit dem Infinitiv**.

   Vergleiche:
   "I**'m going to stop** smoking right now!" (fester Vorsatz)
   "I**'ll stop** smoking when you do!" (Versprechen bzw. Vorhersage)

3. Handelt es sich um eine Vorhersage bzw. um eine Situation, die noch nicht durch 1. und 2. abgedeckt wird, dann ist die Konstruktion mit ***will/won't* + Infinitiv** richtig, z. B.:

   Vorhersage: "Snow **will fall** in many areas tonight."

Neutrale Frage:	"When **will** you **be** back?"
Spontane Entscheidung:	"I **won't** wait for Tom."
Im Hauptsatz bei Satzgefügen mit *if* und *when* im Nebensatz:	"When/If you go I'**ll** go with you."

Verwechsle das englische *will* nicht mit dem deutschen „will":

Ich will hingehen.	I **want to** go there.
Willst du mitkommen?	**Do you want to** come with me?

1

Lies den folgenden Dialog durch und schreibe dann die Sätze, die zukünftige Handlungen ausdrücken, in der jeweiligen Spalte auf:

Peter: What are you going to do this summer, Claire?
Claire: My parents haven't decided yet. But I expect we'll go to the seaside again.
Peter: John and I are going camping in Turkey this year.
Claire: That sounds great, but won't you need a lot of special equipment?
Peter: No. Last year we went camping in France and we had far too much in our rucksacks. We won't take more than we need this time! We're going to fly to Istanbul so 20 kilos of luggage will have to be enough.
Claire: Is John coming to the youth club tonight?
Peter: I'm not sure, but I'm seeing him after school, so I'll ask him. Why?
Claire: Well, I'm going to bring Barbara with me, and she wants to talk to John.
Peter: OK. I'll phone you when I've seen him. Will you be at home at about 6?
Claire: Yes. I'm not going to my jazz gymnastics tonight. But you needn't phone. We'll see each other at the youth club, and Barbara is going to come anyway. What about meeting at the café before we go to the club?
Peter: Good idea. I'll see you there at about half past six, then.

Neutrale Zukunft mit *will/won't*	Verlaufsform der Gegenwart mit Zeitangabe	Absicht mit *going to*
…	….	…

2

Everything will be better in the future – so denken jedenfalls der Junge und das Mädchen in dieser Übung. Formuliere ihre Gedanken mit Hilfe der Wortvorgaben, und zwar in jeweils zwei oder drei Sätzen (positiv und negativ) nach diesem Muster:

run on batteries – not need petrol or diesel fuel

Cars will run on batteries.
We won't need petrol or diesel fuel.

2

not go to school – use home computers – listen to lessons and see them on computer screen

1

people use translation telephones – not learn foreign languages

3

people not work – robots do everything

4

have electric walkways – not walk to school / not take the bus – no pollution

5

secretaries not write letters and faxes by hand – speak into typing machines

3

Stell dir vor, dass du eine Fahrradtour durch Nordengland geplant hast. Du erklärst einem Freund/einer Freundin, was du vorhast. Schau dir die Karte an, und beschreibe den geplanten Verlauf deiner Radtour. Verwende die folgenden Verben *take* und *cycle* zweimal, die anderen jeweils nur einmal!

take (2x) **visit** **follow** **walk** **catch**
pay **stay** **cycle (2x)** **not spend** **climb**

Beispiel:
On the first day *I'm going to take* the train from London to Lancaster.
Then *I'm going to cycle* to Lancaster Youth Hostel.

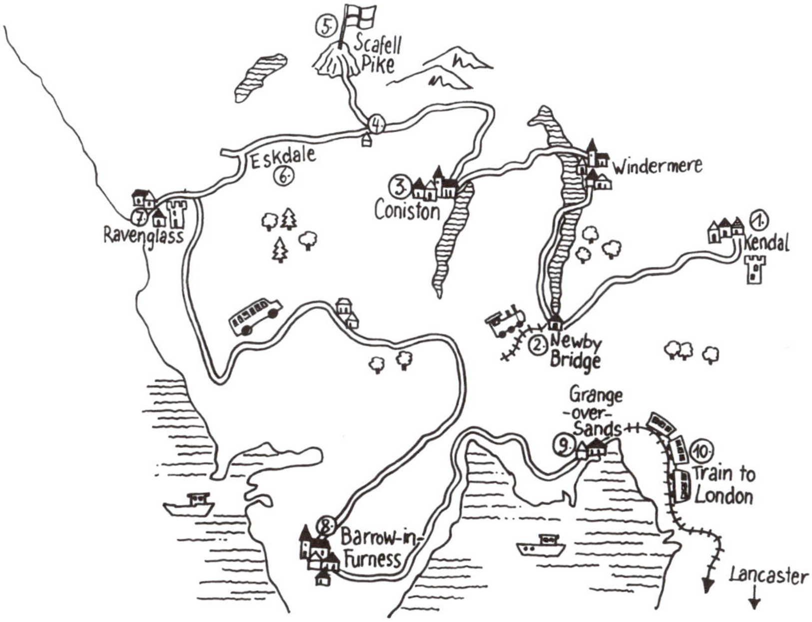

1. On the second day … to Kendal.
2. On the third day … the working railway museum.
3. On the fourth day … from Windermere to Coniston.
4. On the fifth day … at the Youth Hostel near Scafell.
5. On the sixth day … Scafell Pike (3,210 feet!).
6. On the seventh day … a visit to Eskdale and its Roman fort.
7. My friend Alan lives in Ravenglass, so … the night at a Youth Hostel.
8. On the eighth day Alan and I … the bus to Barrow-in-Furness and stay with some friends there.
9. On the ninth day we … the road along the coast to Grange-over-Sands.
10. On the tenth day I … the train back to London.

4

Schau dir den Terminkalender von Frau Schmidt an! Kein Wunder, dass sie wenig Zeit für ein Gespräch mit ihrem englischen Geschäftskollegen Mr Wilson hat! Aber Mr Wilson hat auch wenig Zeit. Sein *appointments book* ist randvoll. Wie kommen die beiden wohl zusammen? Kannst du das Telefongespräch zwischen den beiden vervollständigen?

Mr Wilson:

Monday 2	
Tuesday 3	Computer exhibition – London
Wednesday 4	
Thursday 5	9 a.m. Golf with Mr Makamoto
Friday 6	Drive to Manchester (a.m.) Meet Dr Müller in Leeds (p.m.)

W: Hello. Is that you, Mrs Schmidt? Wilson here. When can we have our meeting?
S: Oh hello, Mr Wilson. Just let me look at my calendar. On Monday I'm … . What about Tuesday?
W: Let me see – No, on Tuesday …, but I'll be free on Wednesday.
S: On Wednesday … our factory in Bremen. What about Thursday?
W: Just a minute – I'm not … anything on Thursday afternoon.
S: What about Thursday morning?
W: Sorry. … with a Japanese customer. Can't we make it the afternoon?
S: No. … a new project with my staff on Thursday afternoon. What about Friday?
W: Friday? Well … in the morning and … in the afternoon. What … on Monday next week?
S: Having a meeting with you – I hope!

Frau Schmidt:

2. Montag	Flug nach Berlin
3. Dienstag	
4. Mittwoch	in Bremen
5. Donnerstag	Nachmittag: Projektdiskussion
6. Freitag	

5

Sieh dir die Bilder an und bilde einen Satz mit der passenden Zukunftsform. Die Wörter über und in den Bildern werden dir dabei helfen.

1. The weather

2. They

3. The boy

4. Someone?

5. I

6. Flight BE 782

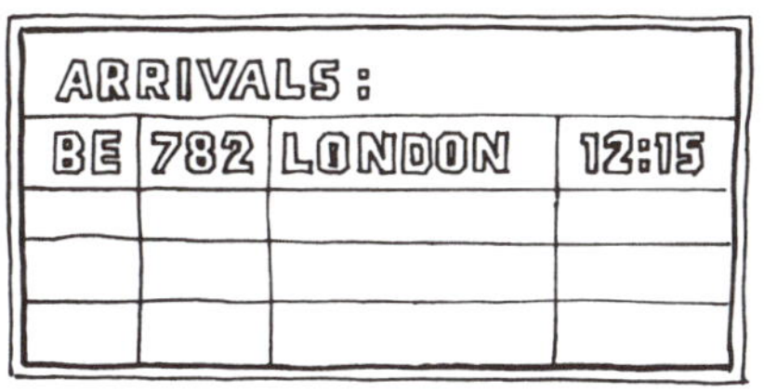

Ways of expressing the future

Zum Ausdruck für Zukünftiges gibt es – unter anderem – folgende drei Möglichkeiten:

1. die neutrale Zukunft	I'**ll fly** to London. Ich werde nach London fliegen.
mit *will/won't* + Infinitiv	We **won't be** there. Wir werden nicht dort sein.
2. *ing*-Form mit Zeitangabe	I'**m flying** to London next week. Ich fliege nächste Woche nach London.
3. Absicht mit *going to* + Infinitiv	I'**m going to** fly to London next year. Ich habe vor, nach London zu fliegen.

Setze in folgende Sätze diejenige Form des in Klammern stehenden Verbs ein, die am besten in den Zusammenhang passt:

1. (see) "Bye, Paul! I'll see you at the disco tomorrow!"
2. (be) "I won n't be at the disco, Jenny.
3. (go) I'm going to the cinema tomorrow.
4. (come) Will you come with me?"
5. (have) "I'll have to ask my mother.
6. (cost) How much will my ticket cost?"
7. (buy) "Nothing. I'm going to buy your ticket. You paid last time."
8. (ask) "Fine! I'll ask Mum as soon as I get home.
9. (be) When will you be at home this evening?"
10. (go) "I'am going swimming this evening, but I should be back at about 9. You can ring me then."

7 Bedingungssätze

If I'd known then what I know now –
I thought I did, you know – somehow
if I could have my time again
I'd take the sunshine – leave the rain!

Roger Whittaker

Wie oft denkt man darüber nach, was wohl gewesen wäre, wenn … ? Aber dann immer diese lästigen Bedingungen, die erfüllt werden müssen! Denn die meisten *if*-Sätze sind Bedingungssätze. Manche Bedingungen sind relativ leicht erfüllbar, andere nur schwer, andere wiederum ganz und gar unerfüllbar. Warum? Das wirst du im Verlaufe unseres dreiteiligen Krimis erfahren.

7.1 *If* -Satz Typ I: Bedingung leicht erfüllbar

Bedingungssätze bestehen aus zwei Teilen: einem Nebensatz, in dem *if* die Bedingung aufstellt, und einem Hauptsatz, in dem das Ergebnis geschildert wird. Die Reihenfolge der Sätze ist beliebig.

Folgende Zeitformen werden für Sätze des Typs I benutzt:

if*-Satz – *present simple	**Hauptsatz – *will + infinitive***
If he wins the prize,	he will be very happy.
if they don't hurry up.	They'll miss the film
Unless you work hard, (unless = if … not)	you won't pass your exams.

1

Suche alle Bedingungssätze aus dem Text heraus. Schreibe sie in eine Tabelle mit den Spalten „Nebensatz mit *if*" und „Hauptsatz". Dann unterstreiche die Zeitformen. Woran siehst du, dass der jeweilige Sprecher die Bedingungen als leicht erfüllbar ansieht?

Sherlock McGnome, Master Detective – Part 1

Sherlock McGnome, the famous Scottish detective, was walking along a dark Edinburgh street. He was going to the empty house where he had hidden the diamonds which had been stolen from the Royal Museum. He had only found them a few hours before, and had just telephoned the King of Scotland to tell him the good news.

Suddenly he heard a voice behind him: "Stop! If you turn round, I'll shoot!" The detective could feel something hard in his back.

"What do you want?" asked McGnome. He thought he knew the voice. "If you tell me where the King of Scotland's Diamonds are, I will let you go." "What will you do if I don't tell you where they are?" asked McGnome. "Then," said the voice, "I will kill you!"

2

Bilde *if*-Sätze vom Typ I zu folgenden Situationen.

Beispiel: *"If I pass my driving test, I'll buy a car."*

1

pass driving test / buy car

2

save enough money / buy dog

3

work hard at school / go to university

4

go to party / meet John

5

get a well-paid job soon / go to Spain for holidays

6

parents allow it / invite friends to party

3

Wir wissen nicht, wie sich Thomas Alva Edison – Erfinder der Glühbirne und vieler anderer nützlicher Sachen – als kleiner Junge seine Zukunft ausmalte. Vielleicht wollte er schon immer ein berühmter Erfinder werden. Vielleicht dachte er sich aber in etwa Folgendes:

Beispiel: Work hard at school – Go to college

"If I work hard at school, I will go to college."

1. Learn a lot at grade school *(Grundschule)* – Go to high school

   ____

2. Go to high school – Learn a lot more

   ____

3. Work hard – Pass my exams

   ____

4. Get good marks in my exams – Get a place at college

   ____

5. Go to college – Study hard

   ____

6. Study very hard – Do well at college

   ____

7. Pass my college exams – Get a good job

   ____

8. Get a good job – Earn a lot of money

   ____

9. Save some of my money – Soon be rich

   ____

10. Be rich – Be able to enjoy life while I'm still young.

    ____

Mehr über Edison im zweiten Teil dieses Kapitels.

Merke
Im Deutschen wird das Wort „wenn" für zwei Wörter im Englischen benutzt: *if* und *when*. Vergleiche:

„Ich rufe dich an, **wenn** ich zurückkomme."

könnte auf Englisch heißen:

"I'll phone you **when** I return." oder: "I'll phone you **if** I return."

Der Satz mit *when I return* ist ein Versprechen. Es ist nur eine Frage der Zeit, bis der Anruf kommt. Im zweiten Satz zeigt das Wort *if*, dass die Rückkehr die Bedingung für den Anruf ist. Kehrt der Sprecher nicht zurück, kann sein(e) Gesprächspartner(in) lange auf den Anruf warten!
Es handelt sich um einen ***if*** **-Satz Typ I** (= leicht erfüllbare Bedingung).

Sätze mit *when* haben mit der Zeit zu tun – die Zeitformen, die benutzt werden, sind manchmal anders als bei Bedingungssätzen.
If und *when* also immer auseinander halten!

4

if oder *when*? – Setze das richtige Wort in die Lücken ein.

1. I'm going to watch TV ________ I have finished my homework.
2. My mother lets me watch TV ________ I finish my homework before tea-time.
3. Please give me the book back soon – only ________ you have read it, of course.
4. ________ we have plenty of snow we sometimes go skiing.
5. ________ we have some snow tomorrow, we'll go skiing.
6. I don't know ________ I'll see him next. On Thursday perhaps.
7. Please come to my party ________ you can.
8. ________ you don't stop shouting, I'll tell your mother!
9. We can go to the disco tomorrow ________ you like.
10. Do you remember ________ the concert starts?

7.2 *If*-Satz Typ II: Bedingung schwer erfüllbar

Auch die Bedingungssätze Typ II bestehen aus einem Nebensatz mit *if* (für die Bedingung) und einem Hauptsatz (für das Ergebnis). Die Reihenfolge von Haupt- und Nebensatz ist auch hier beliebig.

Folgende Zeitformen werden benutzt:

***if*-Satz – past simple**	**Hauptsatz – *would* + *infinitive***
If he won the prize,	he would be very happy.
if they didn't like it.	They wouldn't listen to the music

Viele „Typ-II-Sätze" sind nicht erfüllbar, weil sie sich mit reinen Vermutungen oder gar mit Wunschdenken befassen. Dazu gehört auch der Ausdruck *If I were you* … (An deiner Stelle …).

If I were you,	I wouldn't eat that meat.
if he were here.	He would tell us the answer

Die Form *were* ist für alle Personen gleich:
If I were, if you were, if he/she were, etc.

5

Jetzt aber zum zweiten Teil unseres Krimis. Wie du dich sicher erinnern kannst, wurde der Detektiv Sherlock McGnome gerade von einem bewaffneten Verbrecher bedroht. Schreibe alle Sätze mit *if* auf. Unterstreiche die Zeitformen im *if*-Nebensatz und im Hauptsatz. Sind es alles Bedingungssätze Typ II?

Sherlock McGnome, Master Detective – Part 2

"If I knew where the diamonds were," replied McGnome, "I wouldn't be here. I'd be on the Bahamas writing postcards to my friends. If I had the King of Scotland's Diamonds, I'd be a multi-millionaire!"
"So would I!" said the voice, with an unpleasant laugh. "I know that you have

found the diamonds. Unless you tell me where they are, I will shoot you!" "Don't be silly!" laughed McGnome. "I won't be able to tell you where I have hidden the diamonds if you shoot me." The gunman was silent for a few moments. "Well," said the gunman, not so sure of himself now. "If you take me to the diamonds, I'll share them with you!"
"I don't think you would. If you found the diamonds, you would keep them all for yourself! The game's up, Your Majesty!" cried McGnome, turning round to face the King of Scotland, who looked rather silly now with his walking stick in his right hand instead of a gun. "How did you know it was me, McGnome?" the King asked in surprise. "Elementary, my dear King. Only you knew that I had actually found the diamonds. I had told nobody else."

6

Thomas Alva Edison ging nicht auf die höhere Schule, sondern verließ die *grade school* mit 12 Jahren, um als „fahrender Bonbon- und Zeitschriftenverkäufer" in den Zügen zwischen Port Huron und Detroit seinen Lebensunterhalt zu verdienen. Er war nicht so glücklich über die ihm bevorstehende Zukunft in der Zeitungs- und Süßwarenbranche. Bilde Sätze des Typs II nach folgendem Muster:

Beispiel: More money – Buy a bicycle

"If I had more money, I would buy a bicycle."

1. Bicycle – Not have to walk to the station
2. Not have to walk to the station – Leave home later
3. Leave home later in the mornings – Have more time for breakfast
4. More time for breakfast – Think about new inventions
5. Think hard – Get good ideas
6. Get good ideas – Invent useful things
7. Invent useful things – Soon get rich
8. Get rich – Give up my job on the trains
9. Give up job – Have more time for experiments
10. More time for experiments – Invent even better things

7.3 *If* -Satz Typ III: Bedingung nicht erfüllbar

if-Sätze Typ I und II beziehen sich auf die Zukunft, während Sätze des Typs III ausschließlich in die Vergangenheit zurückblicken:

"If I had known you were coming, I would have baked a cake."

Da man nichts vom Besuch wusste, konnte man keinen Kuchen backen. Auch hier sind die zu verwendenden Zeitformen im Normalfall festgeschrieben: Im Hauptsatz steht die Zeitform *conditional II* (*would have come*, etc.); im Nebensatz mit *if* steht das *past perfect* (wobei im Englischen *had* sowohl für „hätte" als auch für „wäre" steht: *had known/had come* = hätte gewusst/wäre gekommen usw.).

if + past perfect	**Hauptsatz:** ***would have + past participle***
If we had left earlier,	we would have arrived on time.
if I'd known the answer myself.	I wouldn't have asked you
if he hadn't promised to pay you for your help?	Would you have helped him

Vorsicht! „wäre / hätte" ist nicht gleich „wäre / hätte"

Viel Ärger kannst du dir bei einer Klassenarbeit mit *if* -Sätzen ersparen, wenn du daran denkst, dass das deutsche „wäre/hätte" nicht immer *had* entspricht. Im deutschen Hauptsatz handelt es sich um eine Zusammenziehung von „würde … haben/sein".

Vergleiche:

„Wenn ich das gewusst hätte, hätte ich ihn angerufen."
"If I **had known** that, I **would have phoned** him."

„Wenn er nicht gekommen wäre, wäre das Mädchen ertrunken."
"If he **hadn't come**, the girl **would have drowned**."

7

Schreibe alle Sätze des Textes auf, die das Wort *if* enthalten, und unterstreiche die Zeitformen. Sind es alles *if*-Sätze des Typs III?

Sherlock McGnome, Master Detective – Part 3

"If only the King had hired a real killer instead of saving money and trying to do the job himself," said Sherlock McGnome, "I would probably have taken him to the jewels."
"But he would have killed you if you had done that!" cried McWatson in alarm.
"If you had been listening to me, you would have realized that there was never any danger for me."
"Perhaps you could explain that."
"I would never have taken such a risk if you hadn't been waiting at the hiding place, my dear friend."
McWatson looked at the master detective in surprise. But McGnome went on:
"If you hadn't received my note, how would you have known where to wait?"
"Note? – What note? I didn't receive any note!"
"You mean … ?"
"If I had received a note, I would have been there to help you!"

8

Thomas Alva Edison starb 83-jährig im Jahre 1931. Kurz vor seinem Tod mag er auf sein langes Leben zurückgeblickt und sich gedacht haben, wie alles hätte anders verlaufen können, wenn … .

Beispiel: Live in Europe – Not have the same opportunities as in the USA

"If I had lived in Europe, I would not have had the same opportunities as in the USA."

1. Go to high school – Work hard
2. Work hard – Pass my exams
3. Go to college – Not have time to invent things
4. Do well at college – Become a teacher
5. Become a teacher – Never become an inventor
6. Not become an inventor – Not invent all those useful things
7. Become a teacher – Not have to work so hard
8. Not work so hard – Perhaps be happier
9. Move to Europe – Be more successful
10. Die when I was young – Never invent the electric light bulb

9

Bilde aus folgender Schalttafel sinnvolle Sätze:

If …	you hit me	I will help her with hers.
	I knew her address	we wouldn't have lost the match.
	he had waited	you would like her.
	she helps me with my homework	we'll soon be home.
	you knew her better	we would have had a nicer holiday.
	they had asked me to help	we would have taken him with us.
	we walk this way	the girls would bring theirs.
	the sun had shone more often	I will tell Mum!
	the boys brought their CDs	I would write to her.
	we had played harder	I would have done my best.

10

Hier geben wir dir einen Satzteil vor, den anderen musst du mit Hilfe des in Klammern gesetzten Verbs ergänzen. Mal ist es der Hauptsatz, mal der *if*-Satz, der vorgegeben wird.

1. (tell) He … you the story if you asked him.
2. (have) If I … enough money I would buy that computer game.
3. (see) If I … him I'll give him your message.
4. (steal) If he … the car he wouldn't have left it here. He'd have sold it!
5. (call) Unless you stop I … the police.
6. (buy) He … the house if he had had enough money.
7. (not tell) If he … his friends he would never have been caught.
8. (not leave) If her parents had understood her she … home.
9. (not go) We … unless we have to.
10. (ask) If you … me no questions I'll tell you no lies.
11. (want) Tell them I've gone to London if they … to know where I am.
12. (say) Don't shoot unless I … shoot!
13. (not stop) He'll never finish his homework if he … watching TV!
14. (be) If I … rich I'd buy a fast car.
15. (know) I'd have come to your party if I … about it earlier.

Gibt es Kombinationen mit anderen Hilfsverben?
Ja. Das im Hauptsatz verwendete Hilfsverb ist nicht immer *will, would* oder *would have.* Wird *will* oder *would* verwendet, dann tritt das Ergebnis der Bedingung **immer** ein.

If we go to London, we **will** visit the Tower. (Wir werden es tun!)

Andere Hilfsverben im Hauptsatz drücken – an Stelle von „werden" – folgende Bedeutungen aus:

If we go to London, we **can** visit the Tower. (Vorschlag: können)
If we go to London, we **could** visit the Tower. (könnten)
If we go to London, we **may** visit the Tower (gut möglich)
If we go to London, we **might** visit the Tower. (weniger wahrscheinlich)
If we go to London, we **should** visit the Tower. (sollten)

Ähnliche Bedeutungen lassen sich mit Sätzen der Typen II und III ausdrücken, wobei die Wahrscheinlichkeit für die Erfüllung der Bedingung abgeschwächt wird. Die Hilfsverben sind auf *might (have)* und *could (have)* beschränkt:

If you listened to me, you **could/might** learn something.
(da du aber nicht hinhörst …)
We **would / could** be in London in half an hour if we took a taxi.
We **might have** caught the train if we had run faster!

11

Stell dir diese Situation vor: Zwei Minuten vor Abfahrt des Schulbusses rennen zwei Schülerinnen aus dem Klassenzimmer. Zur Haltestelle brauchen sie meist vier Minuten – aber wenn sie rennen würden? … Kannst du ihre Gedanken in Worte fassen? Benutze nicht *would* sondern nur *could/ might (have).*

Beispiel: Be quick! – Catch bus!

"If we were quick, we might/could catch the bus!"

1. Work hard! – Pass your exams!
2. Talk to Jenny! – Invite me to her party!
3. Borrow £20! – Buy those CDs!
4. Phone his friends in Germany! – Get help with German homework!
5. Help your sister! – She would help you!

Bedingungssätze

Bedingungssätze im Englischen verwenden im Allgemeinen feste Zeitformenpaare. Die Wahl des richtigen „Typs" hängt von der Wahrscheinlichkeit ab, mit der die Bedingung erfüllt werden kann.

Die drei *if*-Satz-Typen sehen in etwa so aus:

	„Typ I"	„Typ II"	„Typ III"
Wahrscheinlichkeit:	50 – 99%	0 – 49%	0%

Typ I: Bedingung leicht erfüllbar – kein Problem!
(Wahrscheinlichkeit der Erfüllung 50 – 99%)

Zeitformen-Reihenfolge:
Hauptsatz: **will + Infinitiv** – **if**-Nebensatz: **present simple**

She won't come if you don't invite her.
Will you help me with my maths if I help you with your English?

Typ II: Bedingung schwerer zu erfüllen – bzw. im Bereich der Wunschträume. Erfüllbarkeit bis 49%.

Zeitformen-Reihenfolge:
Hauptsatz: **would + Infinitiv** – **if**-Nebensatz: **past simple**

She would come to your party if you invited her.
If I had enough money, I would buy a Jaguar.
If we knew where they lived, we'd give you the address.

Achtung:
Bei *to be* wird in der 1. Person meist die Form *(I) were* anstelle von *(I) was* verwendet: I'd go by train if I were you.

Typ III: Bedingung nicht erfüllbar, da Situation in der Vergangenheit liegt.

Zeitformen-Reihenfolge:
Hauptsatz: **would have**-Form – **if**-Nebensatz: **past perfect**

I would have helped her, if she had asked me.
If they hadn't come, we would never have eaten all the food.

Setze bei den unten stehenden Sätzen die Verben im Kästchen in die richtige Zeitform. Du darfst die vorgegebenen Verben beliebig oft verwenden. Füge außerdem bei den kurzen Strichen die richtige Konjunktion ein: *if*, *when* oder *unless*.

go not lend come feel promise be bring give

1. "When will you see Pat?" – "This afternoon. I ________________ her your message ________ I see her."
2. "Will you lend me £20 ________ I ________________ to pay you back on Thursday?" – "I ________________ you any more money ________ you pay me back what you already owe me! ________ I ________________ you, I'd find a weekend job and earn some money instead of borrowing it!"
3. "________________ you ________________ to my party ________ I invited you?" – "Of course. I'd love to come. I love parties! ________ you hadn't invited me I ________________ angry with you!"
4. "I think she's OK. I saw her yesterday. She would have gone to the doctor's ________ she ________________ ill."
5. "We could be in New York tomorrow ________ we ________________ by plane." – "________ I had known you wanted to fly to New York, I ________________ my passport with me and gone with you!"
6. "You must show your German test to your father ________ he ________________ home."

8 Aktiv oder Passiv?

8.1 Die einfachen Zeiten im Passiv

Ein Passivsatz bietet sich an, wenn der Täter
- unbekannt ist
- selbstverständlich bzw. relativ unwichtig ist
  oder im Gegensatz dazu
- so wichtig ist, dass er verschwiegen werden muss.

Vergleiche:

1. *Active:*	Someone has stolen **my bicycle**!
Passive:	**My bicycle** has been stolen!
2. *Active:*	Car makers make **thousands of cars** a day.
Passive:	**Thousands of cars** are made every day.
3. *Active:*	My boss made **a serious mistake** last week.
Passive:	Last week **a serious mistake** was made.

Das Objekt des Aktivsatzes wird zum Subjekt des Passivsatzes und so in den Vordergrund gerückt.

Das Passiv wird im Deutschen mit „werden", im Englischen mit *to be* gebildet.

Aktiv- und Passivformen im Vergleich

Active	Passive
Present	
These farmers grow potatoes. *Diese Bauern bauen Kartoffeln an.*	Many potatoes are grown here. *Viele Kartoffeln werden hier angebaut.*
Past	
I bought these videos yesterday. *Ich kaufte diese Videos gestern.*	These videos were bought cheaply. *Diese Videos wurden billig gekauft.*

Present perfect

She has only seen him once	but he has been seen twice in York.
Sie hat ihn nur einmal gesehen,	*aber er ist zweimal in York gesehen worden.*

Past perfect

After he had phoned her …	After she had been phoned …
Nachdem er sie angerufen hatte …	*Nachdem sie angerufen worden war …*

Mit Hilfsverb (z. B. Future)

They will phone him later.	He will be phoned later.
Sie werden ihn später anrufen.	*Er wird später angerufen werden.*
We must tidy up the playground.	The whole school must be tidied up.
Wir müssen den Schulhof aufräumen.	*Die ganze Schule muss aufgeräumt werden.*
I can't find the money.	The money cannot be found.
Ich kann das Geld nicht finden.	*Das Geld kann nicht gefunden werden.*

Bei Verben, die mit Präpositionen benutzt werden *(phrasal verbs)*, kommt die Präposition nach dem Partizip:

His niece will look after him.	He will be looked after by his niece.

1

Lies diese kurze „Geistergeschichte" durch und schreibe alle Sätze auf, die ein Verb im Passiv enthalten. Du darfst die Sätze auch verkürzen. Ordne sie bitte nach Zeitformen.

The old village inn where we spent the night was haunted – or so the local people said. All the other rooms had been booked, so the innkeeper asked us if we would mind sleeping in the "haunted bedroom". My wife did not mind, so I asked the landlord for the story.

"About fifty years ago," he said, "a woman was murdered in the room you have been given. She was found dead one morning, and all her money and jewels had been stolen. No trace of the murderer could be found. Sometimes strange noises are heard at night, so the room is not often used. I hope you are not disturbed. Sleep well!"

We were not disturbed during the night, although I secretly hoped that we would be woken by a scream or the sound of a gun. I began to disbelieve the landlord's story.

We were packing our suitcases the following morning when my wife's wedding ring rolled off the table and vanished underneath the bed.

The heavy bed had to be moved before we could find the ring. The floor had not been swept for a long time, and beside the ring was a bullet from an old-fashioned gun. Had the rich woman been killed by this bullet? We said nothing to the landlord when we paid our bill.

Later the bullet was put in a special glass box and placed on our mantlepiece. All our visitors are told the story of the rich woman who had been killed with it.

Present passive: ...

Past passive: ...

Present perfect passive: ...

Past perfect passive: ...

Auxiliary + passive infinitive: ...

Auxiliary + passive infinitive: ...

2

Bilde Sätze. Hier geht es vor allen Dingen darum, ein Gefühl für die richtige Zusammenstellung (Hilfsverb + Partizip) der Passivformen zu bekommen. Du musst natürlich auch die richtige Zeitform für die jeweilige Situation auswählen.

I Many tourists Mount Everest This car When the news After the band Many new hotels She	am / are / is was / were has / have been had been will be	built so far this year. announced, everyone was happy. made at the new factory. phoned tomorrow morning. introduced, the concert began. stranded at airports last week. climbed in 1953. woken every morning at 6.30.

3

Jetzt geht's weiter – aber vorerst nur mit den beiden „einfachen" Zeitformen. Folgende Sätze wurden alle von *„Dr. Bean's Patent Text Machine"* erstellt und klingen etwas komisch. Wie kann man die Aussagen treffender machen? Achte besonders darauf, dass du im Passivsatz dieselbe Zeitform verwendest wie im Aktivsatz! Eine Umschreibung mit *by* wird in keinem der Sätze benötigt.

Beispiel: People feed the ducks in winter. -- *The ducks are fed in winter.*

1. Somebody often drops rubbish in the playground.
2. A thief stole some money from my jacket pocket.
3. No one likes the new English teacher.
4. My mother burned our supper.
5. A gardener cuts the grass every week.
6. The waiter serves lunch at 1 p.m.
7. An unknown burglar broke into their house.
8. Drivers often break the speed limit.
9. Someone wrote the song "Greensleeves" in the 12th century.
10. Builders build many new houses every year.
11. The police arrested the two young men at the airport.
12. People do not look at these old pictures much nowadays.
13. Does anyone speak English in this shop?
14. Did anything spoil your fun?
15. Nobody expects you to wait.
16. They didn't build Rome in a day.

4

Jetzt geht's mit den zusammengesetzten Zeitformen in längeren Sätzen weiter. Einige Sätze sind in der Frageform, einige enthalten Präpositionen, um ganz sicherzustellen, dass du auch diese „Klimmzüge" bei der nächsten Klassenarbeit meistern wirst.

1. Nobody has seen him since January.
2. Someone will meet you at London Airport.
3. You can buy these souvenirs at any seaside town.
4. After the police had arrested him they took him to the police station.
5. Nobody has explored this part of the country before.
6. Will the judges choose the beauty queen on Saturday?
7. Don't touch that wire! The electricity would kill you if you did!
8. Has anyone ever seen the Yeti?
9. Haven't the police solved the murder yet?
10. They can't have sold all the tickets for the open-air concert yet!
11. You can order the magazine from England.
12. No runner has broken the world record yet.
13. People saw the missing boy in Edinburgh yesterday.
14. After an unknown person had called the police, they arrested the burglar.
15. Nobody will finish this work in time.

5

Vor zehn Jahren wurde in diesem kleinen englischen Dorf der Umweltschutz ganz klein geschrieben! Jetzt aber ist – unter anderem dank der Initiative der örtlichen Schule – schon das Gröbste aus der Welt. Eine Reporterin von der Schülerzeitung hat sich anhand der beiden Bilder Notizen gemacht. Kannst du die Notizen zu ganzen Sätzen ausformulieren?

a) Bilde zuerst Sätze nach folgendem Muster:

Ten years ago a lot of chemicals **were used** on the farms. Now farming methods **have been changed**.

b) Bilde jetzt Sätze im *past perfect* mit *After* … nach dem Muster:

After the farming methods **had been changed**, the fields were / the river was cleaner / less polluted, etc.

Die Sätze kannst du selbst vervollständigen.

ten years ago

now

rubbish put in river: now cleared ✔

many cars parked in village: motor traffic now banned ✔

a lot of coal burned: houses converted to central heating ✔

pollution caused by factory: factory now closed ✔

litter dropped in streets: more litter bins provided ✔

houses made dirty by air pollution: now cleaned ✔

8.2 Verlaufsformen im Passiv

Gibt es auch Verlaufsformen im Passiv?

Ja, für länger andauernde Handlungen – aber nur zwei Formen: *present progressive* und *past progressive*.

Active	**Passive**
They are pulling down the old theatre. *Sie reißen das alte Theater ab.*	The police station is being pulled down, too. *Die Polizeiwache wird auch (gerade) abgerissen.*
Journalists were interviewing the victims. *Journalisten waren dabei, die Opfer zu interviewen,*	while the bus driver was being interviewed by the police. *während der Busfahrer von der Polizei verhört wurde.*

Die Verlaufsform der Gegenwart wird besonders für Sätze gebraucht, in denen die *ing*-Form zum Ausdruck der Zukunft (auch im Passiven) benutzt wird.

Vergleiche:

They are holding the meeting here *Das Treffen wird hier abgehalten,*	but the conference is being held in Edinburgh in two months. *aber die Konferenz wird in zwei Monaten in Edinburgh stattfinden.*

6

Bilde aus folgenden Aktivsätzen die entsprechenden Passivsätze.

1. They are building a lot of new houses in our town.
2. Are they planting new trees in the woods?
3. People are not buying new cars at the moment.
4. Someone was playing a piano at the back of the house.
5. Young people are stealing a lot of bikes nowadays.
6. Was the waiter serving dinner when you arrived?
7. The young mechanic was not repairing my car.
8. Is anyone repairing the roof?
9. Were people photographing the Queen a lot?
10. Nobody is eating all the nice food I made!

7

Nach der einfachen Übung 6 bist du jetzt doppelt gefordert. Manchmal musst du eine einfache Zeitform des Passivs in eine der Verlaufsformen umwandeln, manchmal gilt es, aus einem Aktivsatz einen Passivsatz zu bilden.

1. The famous pop singer John Jones is interviewed several times a week. In fact he ... now.
2. After the heavy snow the main roads were cleared quickly. They ... already when we woke up.
3. "They were still digging the Channel Tunnel when I was in Calais last." – "That's right it ... still ... when I was last in France."
4. While the guests at the birthday party were dancing, their cars (break into) ... one by one.
5. "Am I asking the questions or ... they ... by you?"
6. "They're opening a new supermarket in our village." – "Yes, lots of new supermarkets ... at the moment."
7. The king ... just (welcome) ... by the president when the bomb exploded.
8. "The new boss is making a lot of changes." – "Yes, but I think too many things (change) ... ."
9. "All these improvements (pay for) ... with public money. We're paying for everything nowadays!"
10. "Do you know where the next Olympic Games (hold) ...?" – "I've no idea. Manchester, I think."

8.3 Die Ergänzung mit *by*

Wann muss ich den „Täter" erwähnen?

Eine Einbindung des Täters durch *by* am Satzende ist nur bei Autoren, Komponisten, Sängern usw. unbedingt nötig, denn Sätze wie: *"This book was written"* ergeben keinen Sinn. Alle Bücher werden geschrieben! Der Autor muss erwähnt werden.

Active	**Passive**
The Beatles wrote this song.	The other song was written by the Rolling Stones.
Beethoven composed this symphony.	That symphony was composed by Brahms.
Colin Dexter writes the best written detective stories.	The best historical novels are by Ellis Peters.

Ähnliches gilt für die Ergänzung durch *with* bei Sachen und *by* bei Verkehrsmitteln:

The woman was wounded with a knife.
The dog was run over by a bus.

Wenn mehr Nachdruck auf die von der Handlung betroffene Person gelegt werden soll, wird der Täter durch die Umschreibung mit *by* in den Hintergrund gerückt:

Terrorists killed the reporter.	The reporter was killed by terrorists.

8

Wer hat was gemacht? Bilde einen Satz im Passiv mit entsprechender Ergänzung.

Beispiel: Mount Everest – climb – Sir Edmund Hillary – 1953

Mount Everest was climbed by Sir Edmund Hillary in 1953

1. English Channel – swim – Captain Webb – 1875
2. The first car – build – Gottlieb Daimler – 1885
3. The song "Yesterday" – compose – John Lennon – 1964
4. The Football Association Cup – win – Manchester United – last year
5. Basketball – first – play – YMCA members – in America
6. The novel "1984" – write – George Orwell – 1948
7. The first steps on the moon – take – Neil Armstrong – 1969

9

Hier sollst du selbst entscheiden, ob man eine Ergänzung durch *by* braucht. Natürlich handelt es sich auch um die „Verwandlung" der Sätze aus dem Aktiv ins Passiv, aber du hast jetzt genügend Erfahrung, und die Wahl der richtigen Zeitform dürfte dir keine Probleme bereiten.

1. The boy found the purse in the school playground last week.
2. The girl has already posted the letter.
3. Demolition experts are demolishing the old school.
4. Someone had picked all the apples before I arrived.
5. Nobody can replace the clock he broke.
6. An idiot wrote this letter!
7. He took a taxi to the station because they were repairing his car.
8. Someone must report the accident to the police.
9. The woman who lives downstairs has asked us to turn the music down a bit.
10. Paul Simon wrote this fine song.

Active or Passive?

Verwendung:
Das Passiv wird meist benutzt, wenn der Täter

- unbekannt ist:
  My bicycle has been stolen!
- selbstverständlich bzw. relativ unwichtig ist:
  Thousands of cars are made every day.
- so wichtig ist, dass er verschwiegen werden muss:
  A serious mistake has been made.

Formen:
Das Passiv wird im Englischen mit der entsprechenden Form von *to be* + dritte Verb-form *(past participle)* gebildet. Es gibt nur zwei Verlaufsformen des Passivs.

Simple present	He is seen.
Present progressive	It is being painted.
Simple past	I was / We were chosen.
Past progressive	The songs were being recorded.
Present perfect	The film hasn't been made yet.
Past perfect	John had been seen.
Auxiliary + infinitive	Will we be informed?

Verwendung von *by* zur Angabe des Täters:
- Meist erforderlich bei Autoren, Komponisten, Sängern, Malern – Künstlern allgemein.
- Wenn die von der Handlung betroffene Person wichtiger ist als der Täter.

Wortstellung:
Bei Verben, die mit Präpositionen benutzt werden *(phrasal verbs)*, steht die Präposition nach dem Partizip:

Last night our house was broken into.

Setze folgende Sätze ins Passiv.

1. Someone has invited me to meet the Queen.

   ____

2. The police in Britain catch hundreds of criminals every day.

   ____

3. Nobody told the President the truth about the problem.

   ____

4. The boss will give you a new job when he opens the new factory.

   ____

5. Somebody must tidy up the garden.

   ____

6. They are arranging a Christmas concert at our school.

   ____

7. People had stolen hundreds of things from the shops before someone called the police.

   ____

8. Someone must have warned him that we were coming.

   ____

9. A reporter was interviewing survivors from the plane crash when I arrived.

   ____

10. Elton John has written dozens of good songs.

    ____

9 Der Infinitiv

9.1 Der Infinitiv ohne *to* nach Hilfsverben, *let* und *make*

Der Infinitiv ohne *to* steht nach den modalen Hilfsverben (*can, must, may* usw.) sowie nach den Hilfsverben *will/would* und *shall/should*:

She **can swim**.	Sie kann schwimmen.
I **must speak** to you.	Ich muss mit dir sprechen.
May we **go** to the party?	Dürfen wir auf die Party gehen?
We **will leave** at 8 o'clock.	Wir werden um 8 Uhr losfahren.
Shall we **call** the police?	Sollen/Wollen wir die Polizei anrufen?

Der Infinitiv ohne *to* steht außerdem nach *let* (lassen = erlauben) und *make* (lassen = zwingen).

They **let** him **go**.	Sie ließen ihn gehen. (Erlaubnis)
They **let** him **go**.	Sie ließen ihn laufen. („Sie" = z. B. die Polizei)
She **made** me **wait** outside.	Sie ließ mich draußen warten. (= zwang mich, zu warten)
She **let** me **wait** outside.	Sie ließ mich draußen warten. (= erlaubte, dass ich wartete)

Die betroffene(n) Person(en) stehen dabei als direktes Objekt zwischen Verb und Infinitiv:

Our teacher made **us** stay five minutes longer.	… ließ uns / zwang uns …

1

Setze die richtigen Formen (auch die richtigen **Zeit**formen!) von *let* und *make* – je nach Zusammenhang – in folgende Sätze ein:

1. My mother always … me finish my homework before she … me watch TV.
2. It started to rain and we were still five kilometres from the youth hostel *(Jugendherberge)*. So our teacher … us walk faster.
3. We live in the middle of a big town, so my parents have never … me go to school by bike. They … me walk or go by bus.
4. I was ill when we had our last English test. I hope our teacher will … me take it separately. I think I'll get a good mark *(Note)* for it.
5. I don't like spinach *(Spinat)* much, but my mother always … me eat it all up. She says it's good for me.
6. Big sister: "… me borrow your new CD. I want to listen to it!" – Little sister: "I haven't listened to it myself yet! You can't … me lend it to you!"
7. "Last week our English teacher … us learn twenty-five new English words! I hope she doesn't … us learn fifty this week!"
8. "You're coat is very wet, Eric! Have you been standing out in the rain?" – "Yes, Mum. Our teachers didn't … us stay in the classrooms during break. They … us go out into the playground."

2

Was ist erlaubt, und was musst du tun?
Ergänze folgende Aussagen über deinen persönlichen Alltag:

1. When I get up, my mother makes me ______________________.
2. Then she lets me ______________________.
3. Then I go to school. If it's raining, I must ______________________,
   but I needn't ______________________.
4. Our English teacher lets us ______________________,
   but he/she makes us ______________________.
5. During the morning break, we can ______________________.
   But we mustn't ______________________.
6. When I/we get home from school my mum makes ______________________,
   but then she lets ______________________.
7. Before going to bed I may ______________________.

9.2 Der Infinitiv ohne *to* nach Verben der Wahrnehmung

Der Infinitiv ohne *to* steht auch nach bestimmten Verben der Wahrnehmung. Die wichtigsten dieser Verben sind *to see, to hear, to watch, to notice, to feel.*

I **heard** him **come in**.	Ich hörte ihn hereinkommen.
We **saw** them **drive off**.	Wir sahen sie losfahren.
The citizens of San Francisco **felt** the earth **quake**.	Die Bürger San Franciscos fühlten, wie die Erde bebte.

Wie bei *let* und *make* (s. Kap. 9.1) wird die von der Handlung des Infinitivs betroffene Person als direktes Objekt zwischen Wahrnehmungsverb und Infinitiv eingesetzt.

He watched **a man** break into the house.	Er sah zu, wie **ein Mann** ins Haus einbrach.

Die Infinitivkonstruktion wird bei Handlungen verwendet, die kurz und bereits abgeschlossen sind.

3

Suche das passende Objekt und die passende Handlung aus.

Objekt: two cars someone the car's tyres the Queen the accident a car bomb three masked men someone

Handlung: arrive run explode put scream happen crash shout jump

1. We stood outside Buckingham Palace and saw ______________________ ______________________.
2. I didn't actually see ______________________ ______________________. I was looking in the other direction. I only heard ______________________ ______________________ on the wet road. When I looked round, the car had stopped and the cyclist was already getting up from the ground.
3. The tourist in the crowded market felt ______________________ quickly ______________________ his hand into the back pocket of her jeans. He was probably trying to steal her money.
4. I heard ______________________ ______________________. I looked round and saw my friend Fred.
5. We were watching a motor race on TV. We saw ______________________ ______________________.
6. My friend actually saw the bank robbery. He saw ______________________ ______________________ out of a car and ______________________ into the bank.
7. I was waiting for my bus when I suddenly heard ______________________ ______________________.

9.3 Der Infinitiv mit *to* nach Verben des Bittens und Wollens + Objekt

Nach vielen englischen Verben wird der Infinitiv mit *to* direkt angeschlossen.

I **hope to see** you soon.	Ich hoffe, dich bald zu sehen.
He **wants to talk** to you.	Er wünscht, dich zu sprechen.
They didn't **remember to write** to me.	Sie dachten nicht daran, mir zu schreiben.

Wie bei den Verben *let* und *make* (s. Kap. 9.1) muss jedoch auch bei Verben des **Bittens, Befehlens und Wollens bzw. Nichtwollens** häufig zusätzlich die betroffene Person als Objekt zwischen Verb und Infinitiv eingeschaltet werden.

He **asked me to come**.	Er bat mich zu kommen.
The police **ordered people to stand back**.	Die Polizei befahl den Leuten, Abstand zu halten.
I **warned him not to touch** it.	Ich warnte ihn davor, es anzufassen.
She **advised us not to wait**.	Sie riet uns, nicht zu warten.
They **recommended us to book** early.	Sie empfahlen uns, früh zu buchen.

Bei einigen Verben, die im Englischen ein Objekt + Infinitiv mit *to* anschließen, ist im Deutschen nur ein Nebensatz mit „dass" oder „wenn" möglich:

He **wanted** me to come.	Er wollte, **dass** ich komme(n sollte).
He **expected** me to come.	Er erwartete von mir, **dass** ich kam.
He **told** me not to come.	Er sagte mir, **dass** ich nicht kommen soll.
He **liked** us to be on time.	Er mochte es, **wenn** wir pünktlich erschienen.
He **hated** us to be late.	Er hasste es, **wenn** wir uns verspäteten.
He **preferred** us to be punctual.	Er hatte es lieber, **wenn** wir pünktlich kamen.

Dagegen ist im Englischen bei diesen Verben **kein** Nebensatz mit *that* möglich! Folglich **musst** du z. B. den Satz „Ich will, dass du kommst" mit *I want you to come* übersetzen – also mit Objekt + Infinitiv.

4

Lass deiner Fantasie freien Lauf und bilde neun oder zehn eigene Sätze aus folgender Schalttafel, die du nach Belieben ergänzen darfst! Auch Nonsens-Sätze sind ausnahmsweise erlaubt!

My teacher The soldier The boss The postman The ticket inspector	prefers doesn't want hates likes requested told ordered didn't ask warned advised	his/her pupils passengers me us them	to … not to …

5

Verwende die Konstruktion Objekt + Infinitiv, um die beiden (Teil-)Sätze zu verbinden. Die Verben, denen sich die Infinitivkonstruktion anschließen soll, geben wir dir in Klammern vor. Achte aber auf die richtige Zeitform der Verben!

Beispiel: We're late. Our teacher doesn't like that. **(like)**

Our teacher doesn't like us to be late.

1. "Stand back!" the policeman said to us. **(order)**
2. "Don't be late again!" warned his boss. **(warn)**
3. "Please tell your parents about the school concert," said our music teacher. **(ask)**
4. "Listen carefully," the teacher said to the whole class. **(tell)**
5. The stewardess said it would be better if we sat on the other side of the plane. **(ask)**
6. "Work harder. That's what I expect," said the boss to his workers. **(expect)**
7. Mum: "Don't tell lies *(Lügen)*. You know I hate that!" **(hate)**
8. Father: "Put on a clean T-shirt every day. That's what I want." **(want)**
9. "Learn five new English words a day. That's what I would like," our English teacher told us. **(tell)**
10. "Don't come too close to the fire!" the fireman shouted to the people. **(warn)**

9.4 Der Infinitiv mit *to* anstelle von Nebensätzen

Der Infinitiv mit *to* kann Relativsätze mit modalem Hilfsverb ersetzen. In dieser Funktion drückt der Infinitiv oft ein „sollen“ oder „können“ aus.

Vergleiche:

She's the woman (whom) you should ask. = She's the woman **to ask**.	Sie ist die Frau, die du fragen solltest.
He's the best man (whom) you could take with you. = He's the best man **to take** with you.	Er ist der beste Mann, den du mitnehmen könntest.

Diese Konstruktion wird auch mit Superlativen (siehe letztes Beispiel) und Ausdrücken der Ausschließlichkeit *(the* ***first*** *woman* ***to climb*** *Mount Everest, the* ***last*** *man* ***to leave*** *the sinking Titanic, the* ***only*** *boy in the class* ***not to know*** *the answer)* verwendet.

Wichtig:
Relativpronomen wie *who/whom/which* und *that* verschwinden ganz, wenn diese Infinitivkonstruktion benutzt wird:

He was the last man **who** left the Titanic.	He was the last **man to leave** the Titanic.

Wörter wie *what* (= „das, was“, „was“), *where, how* und *when* bleiben aber vor dem Infinitiv erhalten:

He told us **what** we should do.	= He told us **what to do**.
She asked me **when** she should phone.	= She asked me **when to phone**.
"**How** can I find the answer?"	= He asked me **how to find** the answer.

6

Verwende einen Infinitiv, um folgende Sätze zu verkürzen:

1. "What's the best thing which we could do in this situation?"
2. "I know which (= the) way we should go."
3. "I can show you the best vegetables which you can grow in your garden."
4. There were no houses in which people could live.
5. "I've got nobody I can talk to," said the old man.
6. John was the only one who lost his way.
7. Our teacher told us what we should learn for the class test.
8. "How can I ring Germany from Britain?" he asked me. He asked me …
9. Notice: Will the last person who leaves the office please turn the lights off.
10. "When should I meet you?" she asked. She asked me …

7

Jetzt ein kleines Quiz: Wer hat was zuerst – oder auch zuletzt – gemacht? Benutze die Infinitivkonstruktion in deinen Antworten.

Michael Schumacher — *Edmund Hillary* — *Mikhail Gorbachev*
Boris Becker — *Neil Armstrong* — *Gertrude Ederle*

1. Who was the first person who climbed Mount Everest?

   ____

2. Who was the first German who won the Men's Singles at Wimbledon?

   ____

3. Who was the last person who ruled the Soviet Union?

   ____

4. Who is the only racing driver who has been World Champion five times?

   ____

5. Who was the first woman who swam the English Channel?

   ____

6. Who was the first person who walked on the moon?

   ____

Der Infinitiv

Der englische Infinitiv wird **wie im Deutschen** benutzt:

ohne *to* :

1. nach modalen Hilfsverben, *let* und *make* (= zwingen):

I can **swim**.	Ich kann **schwimmen**.
Let me **explain**.	Lassen Sie mich das **erklären**.

2. nach Verben der Wahrnehmung (*see, hear, watch, notice, feel)*:

They saw me **fall**.	Sie sahen mich **fallen**.

mit *to* :

1. nach vielen Verben, wie im Deutschen:

We hope **to come** to your party.	Wir hoffen, auf deine Party **zu kommen**.

2. nach Verben des Bittens, Befehlens, Wollens/Nichtwollens + Objekt:

She asked **me not to tell** her.	Sie bat **mich**, (es) ihr **nicht zu sagen**.
He recommended **us to walk**.	Er empfahl **uns**, **zu gehen**.

Der Infinitiv mit *to* wird **im Gegensatz zum Deutschen** benutzt

1. bei einigen Verben, die im Deutschen durch Nebensätze mit „dass", „wenn" usw. ergänzt werden, wenn das Verb mit einem Objekt benutzt wird. Die wichtigsten sind: *to want, to expect, to tell, to prefer, to like (= to want), to hate (= not to want)*:

We expected **her to win** the prize.	Wir erwarteten, dass sie den Preis gewinnen würde.
He wanted **me not to win**.	Er wollte, dass ich nicht gewinne.
She hated **people to arrive** late.	Sie hasste es, wenn die Leute zu spät kamen.

2. um einen Relativsatz mit modalem Hilfsverb (besonders *should* und *could*) zu ersetzen:

He's the man **to ask**.	Er ist der Mann, den du fragen soll(te)st.
She's a teacher **to respect**.	Sie ist eine Lehrerin, vor der man Respekt haben kann.

Hier verschwinden Relativpronomen ganz. Fragewörter bleiben erhalten:

"**How** can I get there?" She asked me **how to get** there.
"**What** shall I do?" she asked, so I told her **what to do** and **what not to do**.

Setze die richtigen Verben oder Infinitivformen in folgenden Dialog ein.
Vorsicht! Es gibt mehr Wörter, als du brauchst!

see / to see   let   to come / come   talk / to talk
sit / to sit   understands / to understand   must
need / needn't   treat / to treat (behandeln)

Mr Gifford is a rather nervous old gentleman. One morning he feels ill and phones a friend, who recommends a good doctor. But will Dr Everard see him immediately? He hurries to the surgery *(Praxis)* and talks to the receptionist *(Empfangsdame, Arzthelferin)*.

1. "Good morning. I'd like ______________________ to Dr Everard, please. I must see her at once!"
2. "______________________ me see …
3. I think I heard her ______________________ in a few minutes ago.
4. Do you have an appointment *(Termin)*, Mr …?" –
   "Gifford, Clive Gifford. It's very important. I'm a new patient, but I'm sure Dr Everard will see me. I feel very ill…"
   "Mr Gifford, there are five doctors in the surgery this morning. Why do you want ______________________ one particular doctor?"
5. "A friend of mine recommended her to me. He said she was the only doctor ______________________ all about old people's problems!
6. I ______________________ to see her!"
7. "I must ask you ______________________ down for a minute. If you're so ill, you mustn't get so excited."
8. "You can't make me ______________________ down!"
9. "You ______________________ shout, Mr Gifford.
10. If you want Dr Everard ______________________ you, please sit down and wait a moment. I'm sure she'll see you in a minute."

10 Das *gerund*

10.1 Das *gerund* als Subjekt und Objekt

Das Gerundium wird im Englischen sehr häufig verwendet.
Ihm entspricht im Deutschen häufig ein (substantivierter) Infinitiv.

	Englisch	Deutsch
1. **Gerund als Subjekt**	Swimming is fun.	(Das) Schwimmen macht Spaß.
– mit Erweiterung	Swimming in the sea is fun.	Das Schwimmen im Meer/Im Meer zu schwimmen, macht Spaß.
– mit eigenem Objekt	Eating ice-cream is fun.	Eis essen macht Spaß. (Hier hört's im Deutschen mit dem *gerund* schon auf.)
2. **Gerund als Objekt**	I like swimming.	Ich schwimme gern.
– nach bestimmten Verben	I prefer skiing to swimming.	Ich ziehe das Skilaufen dem Schwimmen vor.
– mit Erweiterung	We like swimming in the sea.	Wir schwimmen gern im Meer. (Kein *gerund* möglich im Deutschen.)
– mit eigenem Objekt	She hates eating cabbage.	Sie hasst es, Kohl zu essen./Sie isst ungern Kohl.
	I prefer reading books to writing letters.	Ich lese lieber Bücher, als dass ich Briefe schreibe.

Besonders häufig wird das *gerund* im Englischen **nach folgenden Verben** benutzt: *to enjoy, to finish, to like, to love, to hate, to prefer, to not mind (I don't mind ...-ing), to go (shopping, swimming, etc.), to be keen on* (etwas sehr gerne machen), *to be mad about* (verrückt danach sein) etc.

1

Lies den folgenden Text durch und unterstreiche erstens alle *ing*-Formen und zweitens – in einer anderen Farbe – die Wörter, welche das jeweilige *gerund* ergänzen, z. B. *skateboarding for young people, injuring other people* usw.

Fun on 4 wheels only?

Skateboarding is popular with young people all over the world. Skateboarding is not like skiing as it can be done in most places and at most times of the year. But if you do not like skateboarding, what about windsurfing or snowboarding? You need the right equipment, of course, and the right conditions – water and wind or snow – but there is less risk of hurting yourself and less danger of injuring other people, too. Many young people have the chance of learning to windsurf when they go on their summer holidays. But you should not go windsurfing if you are not fond of swimming! Most beginners spend more time climbing out of the water than standing on their boards, but after mastering the basic techniques you will usually become quite good at staying on your board and may enjoy windsurfing on the sea almost as much as skateboarding in the city.

2

Bilde acht Sätze mit Hilfe der folgenden Schalttafel. Du kannst, wenn's dir Spaß macht, auch fünf Unsinnssätze bilden. Wir geben die lustigsten Varianten in den Lösungen mit an.

Swimming Walking Reading Eating Listening Writing Working Playing	in bed in the sea letters to friends in the garden the car to good music …	is one of my is not among my	hobbies. bad habits. interests. weekend activities

3

Was meinst du? Schau dir die dargestellten Tätigkeiten an und sage, was du davon hältst.

Beispiel: "Dancing is fantastic/stupid/a waste of time."
oder: "Swimming in the sea is a hobby of mine."

Benutze folgende Wörter für Tätigkeiten, die du magst:

fun / fantastic / super / wonderful / a hobby of mine / terrific / easy

Benutze folgende Wörter für Tätigkeiten, die du nicht magst:

boring / terrible / stupid / a waste of time / dangerous / horrible / difficult

dancing

swimming

hang-gliding

playing football

learning English

cooking

making models

writing letters

cycling

camping

4

Benutze die hier vorgegebenen Satzteile, um deine eigenen Vorlieben und Abneigungen auszudrücken.

1. I like ______________________-ing (…)
2. I don't mind ______________________-ing (…)
3. I hate ______________________-ing (…)
4. I prefer ______________________-ing to ______________________-ing
5. I'm keen on ______________________-ing (…)
6. I'm not so keen on ______________________-ing (…)
7. I love ______________________-ing (…)
8. I'm (not) mad about ______________________-ing (…)

5

a) Schau dir die Schilder an, und bilde Befehle mit dem *gerund* nach dem Muster *"No … ing"*

b) Bilde ganze Sätze, welche die Bedeutung der Schilder erklären:
"No …-ing" means that you can't/it's forbidden to/you're not allowed to …

10.2 Das *gerund* nach Präpositionen

Wie ein Substantiv kann auch ein gerund im Englischen nach einer Präposition stehen. Nach bestimmten Verben, Substantiven und Adjektiven, die fest mit einer Präposition verbunden sind, folgt meist das *gerund* : Im Deutschen wird eine andere Konstruktion (meist mit Infinitiv) benutzt.

	Englisch	**Deutsch**
Nur Präposition	I'm **for** going to the disco.	Ich bin dafür, dass wir in die Disco gehen.
	She's **against** smoking.	Sie ist gegen das Rauchen.
	Instead **of** waiting ….	Statt … zu warten …
Verb + Präposition	He **went on** speaking.	Er sprach weiter.
	She **kept on** asking for my address.	Sie hörte nicht auf, nach meiner Adresse zu fragen.
	They **succeeded in** reaching the bank.	Es gelang ihnen, das Ufer zu erreichen.
	I'm **looking forward to** going to England.	Ich freue mich auf meine Reise nach England.
Substantiv + Präposition	There's no **risk of** losing your way.	Du kannst dich unmöglich verlaufen.
	Is there any **chance of** borrowing that CD?	Gibt es eine Chance, dass …
Substantiv ohne Präposition	It's no **use** asking him.	Es hat keinen Zweck, …
	There's no **point** waiting.	Es hat keinen Sinn, zu …
Adjektiv + Präposition	Are you **interested in** windsurfing?	Bist du an Windsurfen interessiert?
	I'm **fond of** eating rice.	Ich esse gern Reis.
Adjektiv + Ergänzung	He's not **used to** driving on the left.	Er ist es nicht gewohnt, links zu fahren.
Adjektiv + eigenes Objekt	Are they **good at** learning languages?	Sind sie im Fremdsprachenlernen gut?

6

Setze die richtige Form der unten aufgeführten Wörter in den folgenden Text ein. Es wird nicht immer möglich sein, ein *gerund* zu verwenden. Bei Bedarf muss das *gerund* auch durch die entsprechende Präposition ergänzt werden (= „Doppellücke").

lie persuade talk take stay swim
let go spend skateboard swim allow

It was June, and John was already looking forward ______ ______________ on holiday. His parents wanted ______________________ three weeks at the seaside again, but John was not keen ______ ____________________ on the beach in the sun. He preferred ______________________ to ________________________ in the sea. He was not very good ______ ______________________. There was no chance ______ ______________________ at home while his parents were on holiday, so John asked his father if he could ______________________ his skateboard with him. At first his father was against ____________________ John to take such a big thing in the car with them, but finally John succeeded ______ ______________________ his mother ____________________ to his father. At last John's dad agreed ______________________ John take his skateboard. When they put their luggage into the car, there was only just room for John's skateboard. "It's a good job you haven't got a surfboard, John," his dad said.

Das *gerund*

Das *gerund* wird wie im Deutschen verwendet:

Als Subjekt:	Skiing is fun.	Das Skilaufen macht Spaß.
Als Objekt:	I like skiing.	Ich mag das Skilaufen.

Das *gerund* wird – zum Teil anders als im Deutschen – mit Erweiterungen verwendet:

Als Subjekt:	Skiing in the mountains is fun.	Das Skilaufen in den Bergen macht Spaß.
Als Objekt:	I like swimming in the sea.	Ich schwimme gern im Meer.

Das *gerund* wird – im Gegensatz zum Deutschen – nach Präpositionen (auch Verb, Substantiv und Adjektiv + Präposition) benutzt:

She's for waiting.	Sie ist dafür, dass wir warten.
He's looking forward to coming.	Er freut sich darauf, dass er kommt.
I'm afraid of losing my way.	Ich habe Angst davor, mich zu verlaufen.
We have no chance of winning.	Wir haben keine Chance zu gewinnen.

Eigentlich war der letzte Englischtest gar nicht so schwierig, trotzdem hat Katja eine 5 geschrieben. Nur zwei ihrer zehn Sätze waren richtig. Verbessere die acht falschen Sätze und mache nur bei den zwei richtigen einen Haken im Kästchen! Also aufgepasst!

1. She prefers roller-skating to skateboard. ☐

___

2. Sing is one of my hobbies. ☐

___

3. I enjoy to learn English. ☐

___

4. She succeeded in passing her exam. ☐

___

5. We're not used to learn ten new English words a day. ☐

___

6. It's no use to ask him. He doesn't know the answer. ☐

___

7. Instead to wait we should leave right away. ☐

___

8. She's looking forward to get an e-mail from her pen-friend. ☐

___

9. "No, I'm not at all interested to meet you at the disco!" ☐

___

10. They love eating fish and chips. ☐

___

11 Die modalen Hilfsverben

11.1 *Must* und *needn't*

Die modalen Hilfsverben *(modal auxiliaries)* dienen zum Ausdruck von Fähigkeiten, Möglichkeiten, Verpflichtungen usw.

must

German	**English auxiliary**	**substitute**	
müssen	–	to have to	We will have to wait.
muss	I must	I have to	He must/has to go now.
muss nicht	I needn't	I don't have to	I don't have to wait.
musste	–	she had to	She had to go.
gemusst	–	I have had to	I've often had to wait.

Achtung:
mustn't = *darf nicht*: You mustn't drink whisky!

needn't und *to need*

needn't heißt „nicht müssen, nicht brauchen", kommt aber **nur in dieser Präsensform** vor.

Was heißt dann „Ich brauchte nicht"? Hier bedienen wir uns des Vollverbs *to need* (= brauchen), das meist mit Gegenständen benutzt wird:

You need a new bike!
We needed money.
Did you need to ask permission?
She didn't need a book.
You didn't need to come.

1

Setze die richtige Form – oder Ersatzform – von *must* ein.

1. "I must go to the dentist's soon." – "I ____________ go last week."
2. "____________ we do this exercise?" – "Yes, of course you ____________!"
3. "You ____________ eat all the food. John hasn't had any yet."
4. "Do you ____________ go to the meeting?" – "No, we ____________ go if we don't want to."
5. "We'll ____________ ask our teacher."
6. She has plenty of money. She does not ____________ go to work.
7. She did not ____________ take the job, but she wanted to.
8. We have never ____________ work so hard before!
9. I cannot do it myself. You will ____________ help me.
10. I can do it myself. You ____________ help me.

2

Setze das entsprechende Hilfsverb *mustn't* (nicht dürfen) oder *needn't* (nicht müssen) in die Lücken ein.

1. You can have one of these cakes, but those are for the party this evening. You ____________ eat them.
2. There's a meeting of the football club after school this evening, but it isn't important, so we ____________ go.
3. The match starts at 3 o'clock, so we ____________ be late.
4. You ____________ phone me. I'll see you at the youth club later.
5. I've got a map, so you ____________ buy one.
6. The traffic lights are red. You ____________ cross the street.
7. We ____________ wait for Sally. She can't come.
8. We ____________ wait any longer for John or we'll be late.
9. You ____________ shout. You'll wake the baby.
10. You ____________ shout! I'm not deaf!

11.2 *can / could* und *may / might*

can / could

German	English auxiliary	substitute	
können	–	to be able to	He won't be able to go.
er kann	he can	he is able to	I can/am able to swim.
ich konnte	–	I was able to	We were able to leave
sie konnte nicht	she couldn't	she wasn't able to	She wasn't able to/ couldn't come.
er könnte	he could	–	He could come with us.
gekonnt	–	we have been able to	She hasn't been able to write until now.

may / might

German	English auxiliary	substitute	
dürfen	–	to be allowed to	We will be allowed to go.
Darf ich?	May I?	Am I allowed to?	May we touch them?/ Are we allowed to touch them?
er darf nicht	he may not/ must not	he isn't allowed to	You may/must not park here. You aren't allowed to park here.
ich durfte	–	I was allowed to	We weren't allowed to wait.
sie dürfte	she might	–	She might be about 17.
(= sollte)	she should	–	She should be home by now.
Dürfte ich?	Might I?	–	Might I ask you a question?

3

Hier sind drei kurze Dialoge: Junge Leute planen ihre Woche. Kannst du die Sätze richtig ergänzen?

1. "I can't see you tomorrow evening, but I'll … see you in the afternoon."
2. "What a pity. I had hoped that we would … meet tonight."
3. "Well – I suppose I … see you tonight if it was really important."

4. "I'm sorry I haven't … call you until now."
5. "Why … n't you phone me at the weekend?" – "Because we were away."
6. "… you … come to my party on Friday?" -"I … n't … tell you until tomorrow."

7. "If I promised to help you with your English homework tonight, … you … help me with my maths before the test on Thursday?
8. I … only … answer five questions in the last test."
9. "I don't think I'll … help you before Wednesday. Is that OK?"
10. "I don't see why you … help me tonight, when I have finished helping you with your English!"

4

Jetzt eine kleine Übersetzungsübung zu *may*. Du besuchst mit einem Freund einen kleinen Privatzoo in England. Dein Freund fragt, was er alles machen darf. Du stellst die Fragen auf englisch an ein Mädchen, das dort arbeitet.

„Guck mal! Kleine Ziegen. Dürfen wir die Ziegen streicheln?"

1. You: "… we stroke the goats, please?"
2. Girl: "Yes of course. You … to stroke all the animals in this part of the zoo."

„Ist es erlaubt, die Affen zu füttern?"

3. You: "My friend wants to know if it … to feed the monkeys."
4. Girl: "Of course you may. But you are only … to feed them with food you buy here."

„In Hamburg durften wir unsere eigenen Erdnüsse verfüttern!"

5. You: "My friend says that in Hamburg we … to feed them our own peanuts."
6. Girl: "I'm afraid you … not feed your own food to the animals here."
7. You: "OK, thank you. If the weather is good tomorrow, I … come again with a few friends."

11.3 *shall / should, ought to* und *will / would*

shall / should und *ought to*

"Shall we call the police?"	„Sollen wir die Polizei holen?"
"Should we go?"	„Sollten wir hingehen?"
"No, we shouldn't. We should stay at home."	
"Ought we to go?"	„Sollten wir eigentlich da hingehen?"
"No, we oughtn't (to). We ought to stay here."	

will / would

Die Hilfsverben *will* und *would* werden in erster Linie zur Bildung der „neutralen" Zukunftsform (*will*, s. Kap. 6) und des Konditionals (*would*, s. Kap. 7.2) benutzt.

Darüber hinaus können *will* und *would* aber auch zum Ausdruck einer Bitte oder eines Wunsches verwendet werden:

"Will you help me?"	„Hilfst du mir?"
"Would you help me?"	„Würdest du mir bitte helfen?"
"Won't you sit down?"	„Wollen Sie sich nicht setzen?"
"Will you please be a little quieter!	„Seien Sie doch etwas ruhiger!"
"Would you please be a little quieter!"	„Seien Sie doch bitte etwas ruhiger!"

Dabei wirkt *would* etwas höflicher als *will*.

5

Setze *shall / should(n't) / ought(n't) to* in folgenden Sätzen ein:

1. "There's a nice café over there? … we go in for a cup of coffee?"
2. "OK, but we … stay too long. I really … to go home soon."
3. "Look – there's Carl and Elaine. … we ask them to join us?"
4. "Carl? Oh – he … to be here! He told me he was going to London today."
5. "Well, he hasn't gone to London. What … we do? They've seen us! They're coming over here."
6. "Hello, Carl! … n't you be in London?"
7. "London? You … to listen more carefully, Phil. I'm going to London tomorrow."
8. "Well, never mind that now. … we go into that café for a coffee?"
9. "OK, but Elaine and I … n't to stay long. We're going to the cinema.
10. The film starts at 3 o'clock and we … be there in good time."
11. "It's only 2 o'clock. You … n't to be late!"
12. "But we're not going to the local cinema. We're going to the new cinema in the city centre. There … be a bus in about half an hour. But there's always time for a coffee. Come on!"

6

Shall oder *will*? Setze das richtige Hilfsverb in diese Sätze ein:

"What ___________ we do at the weekend?" "Let's have a barbecue in the garden. We can invite all our friends: Tania, Paul, Melissa, Jason, Liza."
"Good idea! ___________ I phone them or ___________ you?"
"I expect I ___________ see most of them at the youth club tomorrow.
___________ Maria be back from Spain by the weekend?" "I'm not sure.
___________ we write her a note?" "___________ you do that?
I ___________n't have time. But what ___________ we do if it rains?"
"We ___________ have the barbecue in Farmer Jones's old barn.
He ___________n't mind." "___________ we ask him if we can use the barn even if the weather is fine? It would be even better than a barbecue in the garden." "Good idea. We ___________ have a wonderful time!"

7

Setze *will/won't* oder *would /wouldn't* oder die entsprechenden Kurzformen in folgende Sätze ein:

John is 16. He has just left school and this is his first interview for a job. Mr Sykes is a friendly man, but John is a bit nervous.

1. *Mr Sykes:* "Come in, John. ________________ you take your coat off?"
2. *John:* "________________ you mind if I kept it on, sir? I'm feeling a bit cold."
3. *Mr Sykes:* "No problem. ________________ you like something to drink? A cup of tea or coffee?
4. Or ________________ you rather have a glass of water?"
5. *John:* "I ________________ mind a cup of coffee, sir. If it's no trouble."
6. *Mr Sykes:* "No trouble at all. (he picks up the phone) Jenny – ________________ you make us two cups of coffee, please?
7. The coffee ________________ be long, John.
8. While we're waiting, I ________________ ask you a few questions."
9. *John:* "I ________________ try to answer them, sir."
10. *Mr Sykes:* "I ________________ be too nervous if I were you! They ________________ be too difficult for you!"

8

Was eignet sich zur Einübung von Möglichkeiten *(can/can't)*, Geboten *(must/should/ ought to)* und Verboten *(mustn't/shouldn't/oughtn't to)* besser als ein Blick ins britische *„Highway Code"*? Auch als Radfahrer solltest du genug über folgende Verkehrszeichen wissen, um mindestens zwei Sätze zu jedem Verkehrsschild zu bilden. Die darunter stehenden Wörter sind als Hilfe gedacht.

 Stop and give way at major road ahead	 Wild animals	 Level crossing	 No right turn
 No overtaking	 Maximum speed limit 30 miles per hour	 Aircraft noise	 River bank, canal or quayside

When I see this sign At this sign	I may not … I must … I can … there may/might be …	I mustn't … I should/shouldn't … (because) … I needn't … I can't … (if/unless) …

Die modalen Hilfsverben

Die modalen Hilfsverben „helfen", die Handlung eines Verbs einzuschränken, indem sie ihr die „Modalität" des Könnens, Müssens, Dürfens usw. hinzufügen:

Can you help me? You **must**!	Kannst du mir helfen? Du musst!
We **mustn't** be late but we **needn't** rush.	Wir dürfen nicht zu spät kommen, aber wir müssen uns nicht beeilen.
You **should** be careful. You **ought to** know that.	Du solltest vorsichtig sein. Das solltest du wissen.
May I open the window? - No. - Well **might** I take my pullover off, then? It'svery hot in here!	Darf ich das Fenster öffnen? - Nein. Dürfte ich dann meinen Pulli ausziehen. Es ist sehr heiß hier drin!

Wie obiges Beispiel zeigt, ist bei den modalen Hilfsverben die zweite Form nicht die Vergangenheitsform, sondern die höflichere, ungewissere Form.

Vergleiche:

Can you come?	Kannst du kommen?
Could your bring Bob?	Könntest du Bob mitbringen?

Will und *would* können auch als modale Hilfsverben verwendet werden, und zwar zum Ausdruck eines Wunsches oder einer Bitte:

Will / Would you help me?	Würdest du mir (bitte) helfen?

Shall wird fast nur in Fragen in der ersten Person verwendet.

Shall I call the police?	Soll ich die Polizei rufen?
Shall we go to the zoo?	Sollen wir in den Zoo gehen?

Was muss ich sonst über diese Verben wissen?

- Mit Ausnahme von *ought to* wird der Infinitiv **ohne *to*** benutzt.
- Die modalen Hilfsverben haben keine Verlaufsformen.
- Um die Vergangenheit oder andere Zeitformen auszudrücken, musst du die entsprechende Form des Ersatzverbs *(substitute)* benutzen, z. B.:

Simple past:	I **had to** come.	Ich musste kommen.
Present perfect:	We'**ve been able to** stop.	Wir haben anhalten können.
Future:	They **won't be allowed to** stay.	Sie werden nicht bleiben dürfen.

Nicht vergessen:

You **mustn't** park here. = Du **darfst** hier **nicht** parken.
You **needn't** wait for me. = Du **musst nicht** auf mich warten.

Füge das richtige Hilfsverb in folgende Sätze ein. Jedes Verb darf nur einmal benutzt werden:

might can't ought should may couldn't shall needn't must mustn't

In the street outside the school playground, a pupil is practising skateboarding. A teacher comes round a corner and nearly falls over the pupil.

1. "Be careful! Why __________ you watch where you're going? You nearly knocked me over!
2. Don't you know that you __________ use a skateboard in the playground?"
3. "I'm sorry. And you __________ shout at me. I'm outside the playground.
4. And this is a play street. You __________ to know that. You're a teacher!"
5. "All right. But you __________ keep your eyes open in future."
6. "Keep my eyes open? You came round a corner! I __________ see you!"

Sonja has lost her keys. She asks her brother if he has seen them.

7. "I've no idea where they are. They __________ be anywhere!
8. __________ I help you look for them?"
9. "Thanks. They __________ be somewhere here in my room."
10. "There they are! On your desk! Right in front of your nose. __________ I make a suggestion *(Vorschlag)*, Sis?" – "What?" – "Get yourself some new glasses." She throws a book at him. "Ouch!"

12 Die indirekte Rede

Bei der indirekten Rede *(reported speech)* im Englischen heißt es immer „eine Zeitstufe zurück, wenn die Einleitung der nichtwörtlichen Rede in der Vergangenheit steht“ – z. B.: *he said, she told me, they asked us* usw. Bei Befehlen gestaltet sich die ganze Sache etwas einfacher. Deshalb fangen wir damit an.

12.1 Indirekte Befehle

"Stop!"	The policeman ordered us to stop.
"Don't move!"	The man told us not to move.
"Never lie to me!"	She told/warned me never to lie to her.
"Please wait for us."	Our friends asked us to wait for them.

Bei richtigen Befehlen nimmst du am besten *order*, bei Aufforderungen mit *please* ein Einführungsverb wie *ask*. Beim „freundlichen“ Ermahnen ist *tell* oder *warn* geeigneter als *command/order*, und beim „Bitten und Betteln“ nimmst du am besten *invite* oder *beg*.

Aufforderungen nach dem Muster *„No talking, please.“* werden auch mit *not* + Infinitiv wiedergegeben: *He asked us not to talk.*

1

Lies den folgenden Text durch und unterstreiche die indirekten Befehle.

The Big Black Bag

I had only been in England for five minutes when I experienced my first bomb scare. Our teacher had told us to keep our hand baggage with us at all times and not to leave anything on the plane.
A voice over the loudspeakers requested us to report any unattended bags or suitcases and not to touch them.
It was while we were waiting for our suitcases that I saw the Big Black Bag. There was nobody standing near it, and after watching it for five minutes

I decided that it was certainly "unattended". A policeman was walking by and I stopped him ... Within minutes a calm voice over the loudspeakers was ordering us not to panic but to leave the baggage area quietly. The voice also asked us to take all our personal baggage with us. Our baggage had not arrived yet, so our teacher told us to leave the baggage hall without it.
We waited outside for two hours. The voice over the loudspeaker invited us to have a cup of tea and a cake at the airport's expense, but not many of us were hungry or thirsty. We were far more interested in the Big Black Bag. Again the loudspeakers warned us not to get too close to the building and to stay away from the windows and glass doors.
Finally we were requested to return to the baggage hall and collect our suitcases. "Ladies and Gentlemen," the voice went on, "the police tell us that there was no danger after all, but we would like to thank the young lady who reported this piece of unattended baggage." My whole class looked at me, and many other people did, too. I had made them all two hours late!

2

Auf dem Flug nach London wurden verschiedene Anweisungen gegeben. Wie würdest du sie weiterberichten? Benutze passende Einführungsverben.

Beispiel: Teacher: "Stay together in a group!"

Our teacher told us to stay together in a group.

1. Teacher: "Don't wander about!"
2. At the check-in counter: "Please put your baggage on the scales (Waage)."
3. Passport officer: "Show me your passport."
4. Assistant in duty-free shop: "Show me your boarding pass, please."
5. Stewardess: "Passengers in seats 1 – 40 please board now."
6. Steward: "All passengers fasten your seat-belts for take-off."
7. Captain: "Please listen carefully to the safety instructions."
8. Stewardess: "No smoking in the toilets!"

12.2 Indirekte Aussagen

Indirekte Aussagen

1. Einführungsverb im *present tense* oder *present perfect:*

direkte Rede	**indirekte Rede**
"I live in Berlin."	He says (that) he lives in Berlin.
"I lived in Berlin ten years ago."	He says (that) he lived in Berlin ten years ago.
"I have never been there."	He has often told me (that) he has never been there.

Nach einem Einführungsverb im *present tense* oder im *present perfect* *(he says, he has often told me (that) ...)* gibt es keine Zeitverschiebung! Die Zeiten der direkten Rede werden beibehalten.
Man kann die Konjunktion *that* bei indirekten Aussagen weglassen.

2. Einführungsverb im *past tense:*

direkte Rede	**indirekte Rede**
"I live in Berlin."	He said he lived in Berlin.
"I lived in Berlin ten years ago."	He said he had lived in Berlin ten years ago.
"I have never been there."	He said he had never been there.

Berichtet man über eine Unterhaltung, die in der Vergangenheit stattfand und deshalb mit einem Einführungsverb im *past tense (he said, she told me* usw.) eingeleitet wird, werden die in der direkten Rede verwendeten Zeitformen um einen Schritt in die Vergangenheit zurückverschoben.

Personen, die in der direkten Rede erwähnt werden, müssen meist in der indirekten Rede geändert werden:

"**I** live in Berlin."	She says **she** lives in Berlin.

Vorvergangenheit ⟵ **Vergangenheit** ⟵ **Gegenwart**

> *I live in London, but I am working in Berlin for six months. I have been in Berlin for two months and can give you my address if you will lend me a pen. I haven't brought one with me.*

She said she lived in London but was working in Berlin for six months. She told me she had been in Berlin for two months and could give me her address if I would lend her a pen, because she hadn't brought a pen with her.

> *I lived in New York for six years. While I was living there I met a lot of nice people.*

She said she had lived in New York for six years and that while she had been living there she had met a lot of nice people.

> *After I had lived in New York for six years I moved back to London and my family and I have been living there ever since.*

She went on to say that after she had left New York she had moved back to London and had been living there ever since.

Merke:
Nach einem Einführungsverb im *past tense* kommen somit **nur zwei Zeitformen** vor:

1. *past tense* (auch bei zeitformbildenden Hilfsverben: *will* → *would*) und
2. *past perfect*

So kannst du die Richtigkeit deiner Hausaufgaben kontrollieren.
Alle anderen Zeitformen sind falsch!

3

Verwandle die Sätze in die indirekte Rede. Verändere nur das Nötigste! Achtung: Eine Zeitverschiebung ist nicht immer erforderlich.

1. "I go to school in London now, but I went to school in Scotland for two years." The girl said (that) …
2. "Your pronunciation is good and you can understand a lot of English." My teacher says (that) …
3. "He phoned my hotel after I had left." The young woman said (that) …
4. "I have no idea what you are talking about. I have never seen you before!" He says (that) …
5. "We are staying at the hotel for a week and so far we've been enjoying our stay." The guests told him (that) …
6. "I want to become an airline pilot so I have to do well at school." She tells me (that) …
7. "We saw him yesterday. He was standing in the school playground." The girls said (that) …
8. "My grandmother has never seen the sea." Our young African visitor told us (that) …
9. "Helena knows the answer but she won't tell me!" He said (that) …
10. "Jim and Vera speak French very well because they've been living in France since 1990." My French friend Jean says (that) …
11. "I was having a bath when the phone rang." She told us (that) …

4

Stell dir vor, du bist gerade in London angekommen, als eine Mitreisende, die nicht so gut Englisch kann, dich um Hilfe bittet. Sie hat ihren Rucksack mit sämtlichen Reisedokumenten verloren. Du musst auf dem Polizeirevier den Dolmetscher spielen. Also keine Verschiebung der Zeitformen. Im schriftlichen Bericht wird jedoch alles „nach hinten verschoben", weil solche Berichte immer mit Einführungsverben im *simple past* geschrieben werden. Schreibe den Bericht anhand des Gesprächs zu Ende.

Policeman: "Can I help you?"
You: "Yes. My friend here can't speak much English. She says she has lost her rucksack."
Policeman: "What's your friend's name?"
You: "… – we're from Germany."
Policeman: "I see. Where exactly did she lose the rucksack?"
You: "At Victoria Station. She says she wanted to change some money

at the station and that she took it off before she went into the bank."

Policeman: "You mean she just left the rucksack there?"

You: "No. A friend was looking after it, but he was talking to some other people and doesn't remember if anyone took the rucksack by mistake."

Policeman: "What was in the rucksack?"

You: "Mainly clothes and a wallet with money, traveller's cheques, passport and so on."

Policeman: "What colour is it?"

You: "Red and grey."

Policeman: "OK, we'll do our best to find it. Where are you and your friend staying?"

You: "Probably at the same youth hostel. I'm not sure. We'll ring you as soon as we have an address."

REPORT OF LOST ITEM

Name and address: ______________________________

Item Lost – red and grey rucksack.

Contents: clothes and wallet with money, traveller's cheques, passport etc.

The owner said she ____________ her rucksack at Victoria Station. She said she ____________ it off outside the bank at the station before she ____________ into the bank. The owner said that a friend ____________ after the rucksack but that he ____________ to some other people and ____________ if anyone ____________ the rucksack by mistake. The two young people from Germany said they ____________ not sure where they ____________ but that they ____________ later.

Modale Hilfsverben in der indirekten Rede

1. Die modalen Hilfsverben *can, may, will, shall* werden nach einem Einführungsverb in der Vergangenheit auch „verschoben“:

   "I **may** miss the train but I **can** wait if you'**ll** tell me the whole story."
   He said he **might** miss his train but **could** wait if we **would** tell him the whole story.

2. Es gibt keine „zweite Form“ von *must* und *needn't*. Nach einem Einführungsverb in der Vergangenheit werden hier Ersatzverben benutzt:

"You **must** leave quickly!"	He said I **had to** leave quickly.
"She **needn't** wait."	The teacher told her she didn't **have to** wait.

   Manchmal werden *must* und *needn't* auch unverändert übernommen.

3. Modale Hilfsverben in der „zweiten Form“ (*would, could* = könnte, *should, ought to*) werden unverändert übernommen, ganz gleich, ob das Einführungsverb in der Gegenwart oder in der Vergangenheit steht – Ausnahme: *could not* = „konnte nicht“!

"We **would** love to go!"	They say/said they **would** love to go.
"She **should** call the police."	He says/said she **should** call the police.
"They **ought to** know better."	She says/said they **ought to** know better.
"I **couldn't** come."	He said he **had not been able to** come.

5

Jetzt eine Übung mit Hilfsverben.

1. "We should take a bus. It'll be quicker."
   My friend said … because …
2. "She can sit in the front of the car. She needn't sit in the back." The driver told the girl …
3. "My friends couldn't help me because they didn't have time." John said …
4. "You must go or you'll miss your train." My friend's mother told me …
5. "I'd like to talk to your brother if I may." The girl said …
6. "I ought to ask my mother if I can come with you." My friend said she …
7. "My sister can't come to your party on Saturday because she is going to London." John told me …
8. "It's going to rain. You should take your raincoats." The guide said …
9. "It might be too cold for a barbecue in the garden. We can have it on the balcony." Dad told us … and suggested (that) …

12.3 Fragen und Vorschläge in der indirekten Rede

Indirekte Fragen

1. Gibt es ein „*Wh*-Fragewort" in der direkten Frage, so bleibt dieses in der indirekten Frage erhalten:

   "**Who** is coming to the party?"
   She wanted to know **who** was coming to the party.
   "**What** is your name and **where** do you live?"
   He asked me **what** my name was and **where** I lived.
   Customs officer: "**Where** did you buy it and **how much** did it cost?"
   The customs officer wanted to know **where** I had bought it and **how much** it had cost.

2. Gibt es kein „**Wh**-Fragewort" in der direkten Frage, brauchst du *if* oder *whether* als Bindewort:

   "Are you German?"
   He asked me if I was German.
   "Did you have a nice trip?"
   Our teacher asked us if we had had a nice trip.

3. *Whether* wird statt *if* benutzt, wenn in der Frage die Worte „oder nicht?" mitschwingen:

   "Have you seen John (or not)?"
   She wanted to know whether I had seen John (or not).

   Man benutzt auch *whether* statt *if*, um unschöne Doppelungen von *if* zu vermeiden:

   "Do you know if there's a bus to London soon?"
   She asked me whether I knew if there was a bus to London soon.

6

Setze die folgenden Fragen in die indirekte Rede.

Beispiel (Satz 1): "He/She asked me what time it was."

Bei den Fragen, die mehr Gedanken sind und an niemanden direkt gestellt werden (mit * gekennzeichnet) sollte *He/She wondered/wanted to know if/ whether/what …* usw. verwendet werden.

1. "What time is it?" (me)
2. "Are you English?" (her)
3. "Were you there?" (them)
4. "Have you phoned Phil?" (us)
5. "When does the film start?" (*)
6. "How much money have we got?" (me)
7. "Did you see Penny yesterday?" (him)
8. "Is the sun shining?" (*)
9. "Where were you born?" (me)
10. "Is there anybody there?" (*)
11. "How much do you earn?" (his friend)
12. "Has Paul phoned?" (*)
13. "Have you ever eaten lamb?" (her)
14. "Where did you go after you had left school?" (us)
15. "What would you like to drink?" (them)

7

Die Polizei sucht eine junge Frau, die letzte Woche in einen Juwelierladen in Mannheim einbrach und Schmuck und Bargeld im Wert von € 125.000 erbeutete. Kommissar Habicht ist gerade dabei, eine junge Engländerin namens Jenny Jones, die kein Deutsch kann, zu verhören. Du musst dolmetschen. Da Verhör und Dolmetschen gleichzeitig erfolgen, werden die Zeitformen nicht verschoben. Nach einer Weile musst du aber auch Jennys Aussagen aus der indirekten Rede rekonstruieren.

Habicht: "Wo waren Sie letzten Donnerstag um Mitternacht, Frau Jones?"
1. You: "The inspector wants to know where …"
Jenny: "I was at a friend's house. We were watching TV at midnight."
You: "Sie behauptet, um Mitternacht bei einer Freundin ferngesehen zu haben."
Habicht: "Wie heißt diese Freundin und wo wohnt sie?"
2. You: "He wants you to tell him …"
Jenny: "Barbara Schäfer, 10, Goethestraße, Stuttgart-Rohr."

	You:	"Sie heißt …"
	Habicht:	"Ja ja! So viel Englisch kann ich schon! Frau Jones, Sie wurden um zehn Uhr abends hier in Mannheim gesehen. Wie kamen Sie so schnell nach Stuttgart?"
3.	You:	"He says you … and asks …"
4.	Jenny:	"I …"
	You:	"Sie sagt, sie habe den ICE um Viertel nach zehn genommen und sei um halb zwölf in Stuttgart angekommen."
	Habicht:	"Und wie ist sie so schnell zu ihrer Freundin gekommen?"
5.	You:	"The inspector is asking …"
6.	Jenny:	"…"
	You:	"Sie behauptet, ein Taxi genommen zu haben."
	Habicht:	"Wie viel haben Sie für das Taxi gezahlt?"
7.	You:	"He wants to know …"
8.	Jenny:	"…"
	You:	"Sie weiß es nicht. Sie hat es vergessen."
	Habicht:	"Warum sind Sie nach Stuttgart gefahren?"
9.	You:	"…"
10.	Jenny:	"…"
	You:	"Sie sagt, sie wollte einen anderen Einbruch *(burglary)* mit einigen Freunden planen."
	Habicht:	"So kommen wir nicht weiter! Fangen wir wieder von vorne an!"

Indirekte Vorschläge

Die Frage *"Why don't we go to the seaside?"* ist eigentlich keine Frage, sondern ein Vorschlag nach der Art: *"Let's …"*. Ein „indirekter Vorschlag" wird meist mit dem Verb *to suggest* + *ing*-Form eingeleitet.

Direkter Vorschlag	**Indirekter Vorschlag**
"Why don't we go/Let's go for a swim!"	Pat suggested going for a swim.
"Let's not wait for the bus."	John suggested not waiting for the bus.
"Shall we ring Jean up?"	Benny suggested ringing Jean up.

Schließt sich der Sprecher aus dem Vorschlag aus, wird das Verb *suggest(ed)* durch *that* + PERSON + *should* ergänzt:

"Why don't you start again?"	The teacher suggested that we should start again.

8

Sieh dir die sechs Bilder an und bilde Sätze mit indirekten Vorschlägen, die dazu passen.

Beispiel: The young man suggested …

12.4 Orts- und Zeitbestimmungen in der indirekten Rede

Wie die Zeitformen müssen auch Orts- und Zeitangaben „verschoben" werden, wenn der Blickpunkt sich ändert. Wenn z. B. an einem anderen Ort bzw. zu einem anderen Zeitpunkt berichtet wird.

Übersetzt man als Dolmetscher sofort jeden Satz, so ändert sich nichts. Berichtet man später, so ist man unter Umständen nicht mehr am Ort des Geschehens. Dann ändert sich die Ortsangabe von „hier" nach „dort":

"I've lived here for years." → He says he has lived here for years.
Später (und an einem anderen Ort) berichtet, heißt es dann:
→ He said he had lived there for years.
Wenn man sich aber noch am „Ort des Geschehens" befindet, heißt es:
→ He said he had lived here for years.
Ähnliches passiert mit Zeitangaben:

"I went there yesterday."	→ She says she went there yesterday.
Am selben Tag berichtet:	→ She said she had gone there yesterday.
Am nächsten Tag berichtet:	→ She said she had gone there the day before.
"We're going there tomorrow."	→ They say they are going there tomorrow.
Später am selben Tag:	→ They said they were going there tomorrow.
Am nächsten Tag berichtet:	→ They said they were going there today.(!)
Zwei Tage später:	→ They said they were going there the next day.

Direkte Rede:	**nach Zeitverschiebung:**
"today"	→ that day
"yesterday"	→ the day before, the previous day
"tomorrow"	→ the next day, the following day
"next week/month/May	→ the following week/month/May
"a few days/months ago"	→ a few days before etc.
"this summer/week/May/year"	→ that summer/week/May/year
"here"	→ there
"in this town"	→ in that town

9

Jetzt machen wir eine kurze Übung gerade zu den Orts- und Zeitbestimmungen. Wir geben jeweils den Ort bzw. Zeitpunkt der Mitteilung in der indirekten Rede an, denn es könnte durchaus sein – wie unser Beispiel zeigt – dass keine Verschiebung nötig ist:

Beispiel: Have you seen John this morning?
(same day): She asked me if I had seen John this morning.
(reported next day): She asked me if I had seen John that/yesterday morning.

1. "How long have you been living here?" – (reported at same place):

   They asked me ______________________________

2. "Is your sister going to the youth club tonight?" (reported later, same day):

   John wanted to know ______________________________

3. "We went to the disco yesterday." (reported two days later):

   Jim and Barbara said ______________________________

4. "We're going on holiday next month." (reported later that month):

   They said ______________________________

5. "I'm going to London next month." (reported two months later):

   He said ______________________________

6. "My mother's going to buy a new car this week." (reported eight days later):

   ____

7. "My class test is tomorrow." (reported later the same day):

   ____

8. "John lives here." (reported in front of the house):

   ____

9. "John lived in this street." (reported at home):

   ____

10. "We saw Paul and Jean a few days ago." (reported the next day):

    ____

Indirekte Rede

Direkte → indirekte Befehle:

"Stop talking!" → He asked/told/ordered us to stop talking.
"Don't wait for me." → She asked/told us not to wait for her.

Direkte → indirekte Aussagen:

Bei Einführungsverben im *present tense* bzw. *present perfect* wird die Zeitform der direkten Rede beibehalten:
"We live in London." → They say they live in London.
"We lived in London." → They say they lived in London.

Steht das Einführungsverb im *past tense*, werden alle Zeitformen der direkten Rede um eine Zeitstufe nach hinten verschoben:
"We live in London." → They said they lived in London.
"We lived in London." → They said they had lived in London.

Die Verschiebung bei Einführung in der Vergangenheit ergibt:

Direkte Rede	**Indirekte Rede**
"live(s)" (simple present)	→ lived (simple past)
"am/is/are living" (present progressive)	→ was/were living (past progressive)
"lived" (simple past) "have/has lived" (present perfect) "had lived" (simple past perfect)	→ had lived (simple past perfect)
"was/were living" (past progr.) "has/have been living" (pres. perf. progr.) "had been living" (past perf. progr.)	→ had been living (past perfect progr.)

"can/could" → could	"will/would" → would	"must" → had to
"shall/should" → should	"may/might" → might	"needn't" → did not need to

Direkte → indirekte Fragen

"Where do you live?" → He asked me where I lived.
"Do you live in London?" → He asked me if/whether I lived in London.

Direkte → indirekte Vorschläge

"Let's go to the disco." → He suggested going to the disco.
"Why don't you go home?" → He suggested that I/we/they should go home.

Bevor du als Austauschschüler nach England gehen darfst, ringen dir deine Eltern mehrere Versprechen ab, geben dir Ratschläge und stellen Fragen. Als du in England angekommen bist, erzählst du deinem Austauschpartner, wie nervig das alles war! Setze die deutschen Sätze in die englische indirekte Rede. In einigen Sätzen geben wir dir eine Starthilfe:

1. *Mutter: Sei höflich* (polite) *zu deiner Gastfamilie!*

   Du: My mother told me ______________________ to my host family.

2. *Vater: Und gehe nicht zu oft in die Diskos!*

   Du: And my father warned me ______________________ too often.

3. *Mutter: Vergiss nicht, uns anzurufen, wenn du angekommen bist.*

   Du: They asked me ______________________ when I arrived.

4. *Vater: Ich hoffe, du wirst eine schöne Zeit verleben* (have a good time).

   Du: My father said______________________.

5. *Mutter: Ich habe an deine Gastfamilie geschrieben.*

   Du: My mother told me ______________________.
   Did you get her letter? – Yes, we got it last week.

6. *Mutter: Ich hoffe, sie können mein Englisch verstehen.*

   Du: She said ______________________.
   – It was quite good, actually.

7. *Vater: Wir würden dich gerne in England besuchen.*

   Du: My parents said ______________________.

8. *Mutter: Wird das möglich sein?*

   Du: My mother wanted to know ______________________.

9. *Vater: Gibt es ein interessantes Freizeitprogramm?*

   Du: My father asked ______________________ leisure-time programme.

10. *Mutter: Wann werdet ihr in London ankommen? Hoffentlich nicht zu spät abends!*

    Du: And my mother never stops worrying about me! She wondered

    ______________________and said

    ______________________too late in the evening!

    Aren't parents the absolute end!

13 Relativsätze

13.1 Relativpronomen als Subjekt des Relativsatzes

Für Personen und andere Lebewesen wird *who/that* verwendet, wobei *that* nur im bestimmenden Relativsatz verwendet werden kann:

Bestimmender Relativsatz
The woman **who/that** lives next door is 84.

Nicht bestimmender Relativsatz
Mrs Jones, **who** lives next door, is 84.

Für Sachen und andere Nicht-Lebewesen wird *which/that* verwendet, wobei *that* auch hier nur im bestimmenden Relativsatz möglich ist:

Bestimmender Relativsatz
The book **which / that** is lying on the floor is "Oliver Twist"

Im Englischen wird ein Komma nur benutzt, wenn im natürlichen Sprechrhythmus eine kurze Pause entsteht. Dies ist beim bestimmenden Relativsatz nicht der Fall.

Nicht bestimmender Relativsatz
"Oliver Twist", **which** is lying on the floor, is my favourite book.

Beim nicht bestimmenden Relativsatz wirken die „Pausenkommas" wie Klammern, welche die nicht notwendige Zusatzinformation von der Hauptaussage absetzen.

1

a) Hier sollst du raten, was mit folgenden Definitionen gemeint ist. Da es sich um Definitionen handelt, sind alle Relativsätze „bestimmende Relativsätze".

Beispiel: A fruit which grows on trees.
= An apple is a fruit which grows on trees.

1. A device which tells the temperature.
2. A person who drives a bus.
3. A person who plays CDs and records at a disco.
4. A vehicle which has wings.
5. A man or woman who works in a school.
6. A sign that tells drivers what to do.
7. A boy or girl who goes to school.
8. A yellow fruit which is very sour.
9. A small, portable roof which keeps out the rain.

b) Jetzt musst du selbst versuchen, gute Definitionen zu geben – natürlich mit dem richtigen Relativpronomen.

who – which – that

Beispiel: A dictionary is a book *which/that explains words.*

1. A passport is a document ____________________
2. Chewing gun is something ____________________
3. A bus is a vehicle ____________________
4. A cat is an animal ____________________
5. An explorer is a person ____________________
6. A walkman is a device ____________________
7. Students are people ____________________
8. A snowboard is something ____________________
9. Rollerskates are things ____________________
10. A ghost is something ____________________

2

Jetzt geht es darum, die „Zusatzinfos“ den jeweils zutreffenden Personen bzw. Dingen zuzuordnen. Verbinde Haupt- und Relativsatz mit *who* bzw. *which* und füge die fehlenden Wörter bei Bedarf ein.

1. Prince Charles	works in a coal mine	red legs.
2. The blackbird	a city in Germany	a world language.
3. John Evans	lives in trees	could ride a horse.
4. The Mini	help sick people	speaks Welsh.
5. English	was a film star	still very popular.
6. Hamburg	was once a large port	is west of London.
7. Flying doctors	is a black mineral	is a large port.
8. Coal	a small two-door car	burns very well.
9. John Wayne	the son of the Queen	has two sons.
10. Bristol	spoken everywhere	work in Australia.

3

Unterstreiche mit unterschiedlichen Farben die bestimmenden und die nicht bestimmenden Relativsätze im folgenden Artikel aus dem *„Croydon Advertiser“*. Du kannst sie natürlich auch in verkürzter Form *(“A teenager who stole …”, “Thornton Heath, which is a suburb …”)* in zwei Spalten aufschreiben.

No 14, Thursday

Croydon Advertiser

Joyrider arrested

A teenager who stole a car in Croydon last week was arrested yesterday in Brighton after a 40-mile police chase. James Wilkinson, who lives at 69, High Street, Thornton Heath, is only 16 years old and has no driving licence. The car which he stole was a blue Morris 1100 that belong-ed to Ms Jane Campbell, who also lives in Thornton Heath. James broke into the car, which was parked outside Ms Campbell's house, and tried to steal the radio. He was unable to steal the radio, which was firmly fixed to the dashboard, but he found a spare set of keys and decided to steal the car instead.

The policemen who followed the stolen car are the same men who stopped two joyriders last month: PC John Laky of Croydon and his colleague, PC Alfred Frazer, who lives in Warlingham. The police car which they were driving was parked beside the A23, which is a busy road that is used by thousands of cars on their way from London to Brighton. PC Leaky recognized the number of the stolen car and began to follow it. The policemen, who could see that the driver was very young, did not wish to frighten the thief, who was driving at about 65 mph, so they followed the car slowly for a few miles.

When Wilkinson saw that the car that was following him was a police car, he tried to drive faster. Luckily the Morris 1100 which Wilkinson had stolen ran out of petrol just outside Brighton. Wilkinson tried to run away, but the crew of another police car from Brighton, which had been waiting near the end of the A 23, caught him.

4

Setze das richtige Relativpronomen *(who/which/that)* in die Lücken ein.

Come to Tenby for a seaside holiday ___________ is different!

People ___________ enjoy seaside holidays will love Tenby. This small seaside town in South Wales, ___________ has two wonderful sandy beaches, is also famous for the castle ___________ stands at the top of the town between the two bays. Tenby is an ideal place for young people ___________ want to do more than lie on the beach. There are many interesting paths ___________ follow the rocky coastline, and for those of you ___________ are not good walkers, there are plenty of places ___________ are worth visiting in the town itself. There are boat trips to the small island of Caldy, ___________ has a lighthouse and a Roman Catholic monastery. Jean Smith, ___________ has been coming to Tenby regularly for over 50 years, says: "Tenby is a place ___________ attracts all kinds of people, old (like me) and young (like my granddaughter), ___________ is here with me this year."

5

Aus zwei mach eins. Füge die beiden Kurzsätze so zusammen, dass ein einziger Satz entsteht. Entscheide selbst, ob es sich um einen bestimmenden oder einen nicht bestimmenden Relativsatz handelt:

1. This is the man. He lives in the flat above ours.

   ____

2. Do you like the ice-cream? It tastes like toffee.

   ____

3. John Brown lives next door. He is a good friend of mine.

   ____

4. She is wearing a long skirt. It is very pretty.

   ____

5. The clothes are expensive. She buys them in Paris.

   ____

6. My girlfriend Alison is 19. She lives in Cleversulzbach.

   ____

7. This is the bus. It goes to Euston Station.

   ____

8 Here are the shoesThey cost me £60.

   ____

9. When did you see the man? He stole my car!

   ____

10. This coffee comes all the way from Kenya. It smells very fresh.

   ____

13.2 Relativpronomen als Objekt des Relativsatzes; *whose*

Relativpronomen als Objekt des Relativsatzes

Für Personen und andere Lebewesen wird *who(m)/that* verwendet, wobei *that* wiederum nur im bestimmenden Relativsatz verwendet werden kann. Im bestimmenden Relativsatz kann ein Relativpronomen, das als Objekt benutzt wird, auch weggelassen werden:

Bestimmender Relativsatz	Nicht bestimmender Relativsatz
The woman **who(m)/that** I saw lives next door. *oder:* The woman I saw lives next door.	Mrs Jones, **who(m)** I saw yesterday, lives next door.

Für Sachen und andere Nichtlebewesen wird *which/that* verwendet, wobei *that* nur im bestimmenden Relativsatz verwendet werden kann.

Im bestimmenden Relativsatz kann ein Relativpronomen, das als Objekt benutzt wird, auch weggelassen werden:

Bestimmender Relativsatz	Nicht bestimmender Relativsatz
The song **which/that** I was listening to was 'Yesterday' The song I was listening to …	'Yesterday', **which** was written by the Beatles, is a great song.

Vergleiche folgende Sätze mit Präpositionen:

„Der Mann, mit dem ich sprach … " =
"The man **to whom** I was speaking … " (sehr vornehm!)
"The man **who(m)** I was speaking **to** … " (sehr korrekt – aber eher in der Schriftsprache zuhause!)
"The man I was speaking **to** … " (korrektes gesprochenes Englisch)

„Der Tunnel, durch den wir fahren mussten, war sehr lang." =
"The tunnel **through which** we had to travel was very long."
"The tunnel **which** we had to travel **through** was very long."
"The tunnel we had to travel **through** was very long."

6

Setze das richtige Relativpronomen ein, aber nur wenn nötig!

The place ________________ I went to for my summer holidays last year was a little village ________________ is difficult to find on most maps of Scotland but a place ________________ you will easily find on a map of Canada: Calgary on the Island of Mull, ________________ is off the west coast of Scotland. The Canadian town ________________ is called Calgary was originally a small fort ________________ the Canadian Mounted Police founded in 1875 as Fort Brisebois, a French name ________________ few of the policemen could pronounce correctly. The fort was renamed Calgary, ________________ means "clear running water" in Gaelic, by Colonel James F. Macleod, ________________ came from the Island of Mull. The year in ________________ the fort was renamed was 1876. The small hotel ________________ we stayed at had a fine view of the bay, ________________, with its blue sea and pure white sand, was ideal for bathing.

7

Lies folgenden Text über die Geschichte der Londoner Untergrundbahn. Welche Sätze können gekürzt werden, welche nicht? Welche Relativsätze können anders formuliert werden?

1. The school project which we did was about London in the 19th century.
2. The teacher who helped us collect material was Mr Peters.
3. Some of the material which we collected was very interesting.
4. Anne Harrap, with whom I was working on the project, is a good friend of mine.
5. Our part of the project was something about which we didn't know much: the London Underground!
6. The first part of the London Underground, which is still the biggest underground network in the world, opened in 1863.
7. Even in those days the streets which connected the suburbs of West London with the banks and offices of the City were overcrowded.
8. This first underground railway, which many "commuters" used, was called the Metropolitan Railway.

9. The name which it was given was taken over by underground railways all over the world.
10. The Paris and Moscow "Metros", which are used by millions each day, are both named after it.
11. The first real "tube" railway on which electric trains were used was built in 1890.
12. At the end of the 19th century there were many miles of underground lines, which most people preferred to the horse buses above ground.
13. Londoners are proud of their Underground. But the man who did most to start up the system was an American.
14. Charles Tyson Yerkes, who had made a fortune in the USA, was the man to whom Londoners should be grateful for their Underground.
15. It was he who insisted on electric trains instead of steam engines in the early days.
16. The Glasgow Underground, which was for many years the only other "Metro" in Britain, had a very small, very dirty circular line with steam trains that lasted until the 1930s!

8

Unser „rasender Reporter" hat zu einigen Ereignissen des Tages nur stichwortartige Notizen machen können. Kannst du sie als ganze Sätze formulieren? Benutze nach Möglichkeit mindestens zwei Relativsätze pro Story.

Beispiel:
Football match – played last night – won by Huddersfield – town in Yorkshire

The football match which was played last night was won by Huddersfield, which is a town in Yorkshire.

1. The new Arrow sports car – made in Coventry – won rally – rally organized by the Automobile Club of Scotland.
2. Boy of 16 – built his own plane – flew 500 metres before crashing into car – parked in the middle of a field.
3. Melissa Ryman – lives in London – will swim for England – European championships – begin next week in Paris.
4. Open-air concert – cancelled last week – will take place next week at Folly Farm – near Oxford.
5. First British spacecraft "Britannia I" – launched next month – will carry four astronauts – chosen from over 1000 applicants.
6. Computer – developed by Irish company will be sold by Eurocomp – has headquarters in Dublin.

1. whose

Das Relativpronomen *whose* drückt Besitz oder Zugehörigkeit aus.
Es wird meistens in Bezug auf Personen oder Tiere verwendet.

Bestimmender Relativsatz:

Darwin was a biologist. His ideas were revolutionary.
Darwin was a biologist whose ideas were revolutionary.

Nicht bestimmender Relativsatz:

This is Peter Piper. I'm sure you know his books.
This is Peter Piper, whose books I'm sure you know.

2. of which

Um Zugehörigkeit bei Dingen auszudrücken, wird statt *whose* meistens das nachgestellte *of which* gebraucht.

Bestimmender Relativsatz:

This is the house. Its roof was damaged.
This is the house the roof of which was damaged.

Nicht bestimmender Relativsatz:

23 High Street had to be demolished. Its roof was damaged.
23 High Street, the roof of which was damaged, had to be demolished.

9

Füge die beiden Sätze zu einem einzigen Satz zusammen.

1. James Watt was an inventor. His steam engine revolutionized industry.
2. Watt was born in Scotland. The capital of Scotland is Edinburgh.
3. This is the rare XL 320 sports car. Only 200 of them were built.
4. The man was very angry. His car had been stolen.
5. The Rolling Stones are still together. Their songs have been best sellers since the 60s.
6. The company is still doing well. Its collapse was forecast months ago.
7. Mr Smith was very happy. His son won the prize.
8. The car belonged to Mr Granger. Its door was damaged.
9. The man was very happy. His daughter won the prize.
10. The villages were cut off. Their streets were flooded.

Relativsätze

1. Ein **bestimmender Relativsatz** wird verwendet, um Personen bzw. Sachen genau zu bestimmen:
   I know the man. - Which man? - The man **who / that** lives next door.

   Relativpronomen im Objektfall können weggelassen werden:
   That book is boring. - Which book? -
   The book **(which / that)** you lent me.
   He was the winner. - Who was? - The man **to whom** I was talking.
   The man **(whom)** I was talking **to**.

   Das Relativpronomen für Personen und Lebewesen lautet: *who/ that*. Das Relativpronomen für Nichtlebewesen lautet: *which/that*. *That* kann nicht nach einer Präposition verwendet werden.

2. Ein **nicht bestimmender Relativsatz** wird benutzt, um zusätzliche Informationen über Personen oder Sachen zu geben:
   John Williams, **who** lives in North Street, was at the party.
   I also saw Julie Wilson, **who** was in hospital last week.

   Das Relativpronomen für Personen und Lebewesen lautet: *who*.
   Das Relativpronomen für Nichtlebewesen lautet: *which*.

   Achtung:
   Im nicht bestimmenden Relativsatz können die Relativpronomen nicht weggelassen werden.

3. **whose** Um Besitz oder Zugehörigkeit auszudrücken, wird in Bezug auf Personen oder Tiere das Relativpronomen *whose* verwendet.
   The man **whose** wife was a painter was a friend of mine.
   John, **whose** wife works in London, is unemployed.

Füge das richtige Relativpronomen in folgende Sätze ein. Denke dabei auch an die wichtige Unterscheidung bei der Komma-(= „Pause“)Setzung. Füge nur Kommas ein, wenn sie unbedingt erforderlich sind. Als kleine Hilfe setzen wir immer dort ein Fragezeichen, wo du überlegen musst, ob ein Komma gesetzt werden soll oder nicht.

1. The house ? in ________________ we live ? was built in 1906.
2. Mr Aloysius Prang ? ________________ built it ? was a rather eccentric man.
3. The materials ? ________________ he used ? were very modern at the time: concrete *(Beton)* and steel girders *(Stahlträger)*.
4. But the brickwork *(Mauerwerk)* on the front of the house ? ____________ looks like most houses built in 1906 ? is only painted on the concrete!
5. Few people look twice at our house ? ________________ my parents bought five years ago.
6. But a year ago an architect ? ________________ had heard about the house ? visited us.
7. He told us he had heard about a house ? the front of ________________ was painted to look like brick *(Backstein, Ziegelstein)*.
8. He was writing a book about architects ? ________________ ideas had been ahead of their time.
9. He said that Aloysius Prang ? ________________ house we were living in ? had been one of them.
10. So now our house is famous! There is a long article about our house in the book by the young architect ? ________________ we talked to that day.

14 Die Pronomen

14.1 Die Formen der Personalpronomen

Ein Personalpronomen ersetzt in der Regel ein Substantiv (Nomen) oder einen Eigennamen – oft um unnötige Wiederholungen zu vermeiden:

"Have you seen **John** or **Mary**?" – "Yes. **He**'s in the living-room and **she**'s in the garden. Do you want to talk to **them**?"

Hier eine Zusammenstellung der Personalpronomen:

Subjektform

ich	*du/Sie**	*er*	*sie**	*es*	*wir*	*ihr/Sie**	*sie**
I	you	he	she	it	we	you	they

Ojektform

me	you	him	her	it	us	you	them
mich	*dich/Sie**	*ihn*	*sie**	*es*	*uns*	*euch/Sie**	*sie**
mir	*dir/Ihnen*	*ihm*	*ihr*	*ihm*	*uns*	*euch/Ihnen*	*ihnen*

* Zu Problemen, die aus der Mehrdeutigkeit von „sie/Sie" entstehen können, siehe S. 140.

Im Gegensatz zum Deutschen gibt es keine Unterscheidung zwischen den Objektpronomen für Akkusativ und Dativ:

"I'm looking for John. Have you seen **him**? I want to give **him** a CD."
*„Ich suche John. Hast du **ihn** gesehen? Ich möchte **ihm** eine CD geben."*

1

Lies diese kleine Geschichte durch. Sie enthält viele unnötige Wiederholungen, die wir in **Fettdruck** hervorgehoben haben. Schreibe die Geschichte in „Kurzform" ab, indem du die fett gedruckten Stellen durch Pronomen ersetzt.

Yesterday **my friend Mary and I** went shopping by bus. The bus was late. When **the bus** arrived, we got on. The bus-driver asked **my friend and me** where we wanted to go. I said: "Tooting Station, please" and **Mary** said: "Tooting, too." **The bus-driver** smiled and said: "Two to Tooting!" The people in the bus heard **the driver**. **The people in the bus** laughed at his little joke. We thought **the people** were very silly. We didn't look at **the people**. We gave **the bus-driver** the money. He took the money and gave **Mary and me** our tickets and our change. He gave me 5p change and gave **Mary** 45p. My ticket said: 45p. Mary looked at **my ticket**, too. Then **Mary** looked at me and I looked at **Mary**. "Excuse me," I said to the driver. "You've given **my friend** the wrong change. She gave you a pound coin and **the fare's** only 45p to Tooting Station. You only gave **Mary** 45p change instead of 55p." **The bus driver** gave **my friend** another 10p. He was not smiling now. All the other people in the bus were looking at **the driver**. "He's given one of **those young people** the wrong change!" said an old man. **Mary and I** smiled at **the man**. "I'm going to Tooting, too!" **the man** said. This time everybody laughed – except the bus driver, of course!

2

Setze die richtigen Personalpronomen ein:

"I've lost my keys, Dad. Can ________ help ________ to find ________?"

"Weren't ________ on the table in the hall this morning?"

"No, those were Mum's keys. I gave ________ to Mum. My keys were in my jacket pocket, but I can't find my jacket. Have ________ seen ________?"

"Your old jeans jacket? _____ think Mum gave _____ away this morning."

"Gave my jacket away? ________ was my favourite jeans jacket. ________ wore ________ almost every day – and ________ wasn't old. Only a year or two, anyway."

"There were some people at the door this morning. ________ were collecting old clothes for the Red Cross. I think Mum gave ________ your jacket – and a few of my old clothes, too."

"But surely Mum looked in the pockets before ________ gave the things away!"

"________'m not sure, Carol. By the way, have ________ seen my old black trousers? ________ were in the bedroom but now I can't find ________. There was a £20 note in the back pocket! Where's Mum, anyway. Just wait till I see ________! I'll give ________ a boot in the head if ________'s given my trousers away!"

Die Entsprechungen für „sie/Sie" im Englischen

Bei Übersetzungen ist es oft schwierig, das richtige englische Pronomen für die deutschen Pronomen „sie" und „Sie" zu finden, zumal du die Großschreibung nicht hören kannst, sondern nur in der Schriftform erkennst! Die Verbform verrät oft, aber nicht immer, die Funktion von „sie/Sie" als Subjekt, nicht aber als Objekt! Vergleiche folgende Funktionen der deutschen Pronomen „sie/Sie" mit ihren englischen Entsprechungen:

Sie *kennt* ***sie*** *gut.*	**She** knows **her** well.
Sie *kennt* ***sie*** *gut.*	**She** knows **them** well.
Sie *kennt* ***Sie*** *gut.*	**She** knows **you** well.
Sie *kennen* ***sie*** *gut.*	**You** know **her** well.
Sie *kennen* ***sie*** *gut.*	**You** know **them** well.
Sie *kennen* ***sie*** *gut.*	**They** know **her** well.
Sie *kennen* ***sie*** *gut.*	**They** know **them** well.
Sie *kennen* ***Sie*** *gut.*	**They** know **you** well.

Die englische Sprache hat für jede Person ein separates Pronomen!

3

Setze im englischen Satz das richtige Pronomen für das deutsche „sie/Sie" ein.

1. „**Sie** ist aus London.	"_______ is from London.
Ich verstehe **sie** gut."	I understand _______ well."
„Wissen **Sie**, wo **sie** wohnt?"	"Do _______ know where _______ lives?"
2. „Kommen **sie** aus Berlin?"	"Do _______ come from Berlin?"
„Nein, **sie** kommen aus Köln.	"No, _________ come from Cologne.
Ich kenne **sie** gut."	I know _________ well."
„Wissen **Sie**, wo **sie** wohnen?"	"Do _______ know where ________ live?"
3. „**Sie** geht in meine Klasse.	"_______ is in my class.
Ich sehe **sie** jeden Tag."	I see _______ every day."
4. „Ich finde diese Bücher gut.	"I think these books are good.
Sie können **sie** überall kaufen."	_______ can buy _________ everywhere."
5. „Hast du Ken und Tom gesehen?"	"Have you seen Ken and Tom?"
„Ja, Ich habe **sie** im Hof gesehen.	"Yes, I saw _______ in the playground.
Sie spielten Fußball."	_______ were playing football."

14.2 Die Reihenfolge der Objektpronomen im Satz

Wie in Kap. 14.1 erläutert, gibt es im Englischen (im Gegensatz zum Deutschen) nur eine Objektform - unabhängig davon, ob es sich um ein direktes oder ein indirektes Objekt handelt.

Bei der Reihenfolge der Objekte im Satz muss dagegen sehr wohl zwischen direktem und indirektem Objekt unterschieden werden.

Folgende Fälle können auftreten:

1. Beide Objekte sind Substantive:

	indirektes Obj.	direktes Obj.
He bought	**his sister**	**an ice-cream**.
Er kaufte	***seiner Schwester***	***ein Eis.***

In diesem Fall steht - wie auch im Deutschen - das indirekte meist vor dem direkten Objekt.

2. Eines der Objekte ist ein Pronomen:

Direktes Objekt als Pronomen:	He bought **it** for his sister.
Indirektes Objekt als Pronomen:	He bought **her** a new CD.

Dann steht das Pronomen immer vor dem anderen Objekt. Dabei ist es egal, ob es sich um das direkte oder um das indirekte Objekt handelt.

3. Beide Objekte sind Pronomen:

	direkt	indirekt
He bought	**it**	**(for) her**.
He gave	**it**	**(to) her**.

In diesem Fall steht meist das direkte Objektpronomen vor dem indirekten. Das indirekte Objektpronomen wird dabei häufig mit einer Präposition angeschlossen - je nach Verb entweder mit *to* oder *for* .

4

Jetzt sollst du die Objekte in die richtige Reihenfolge bringen! Bilde zehn richtige Sätze aus folgender Schalttafel. Du darfst ruhig „mischen": also ein Substantiv mit einem Pronomen oder nur zwei Pronomen. Wie wäre es mit je fünf?

		a new CD	
		her brother	to us
My friend Brian		me	a new CD
I	bought	it	it
Her mum	gave	us	them
You	sent	them	to his sister
They	lent	my friend Jack	for his friend Jack
We		some sweets	a postcard from France
		a magazine	for me
		a letter	

5

In dieser Übung geht es um Objekt- und um Subjektpronomen:
Ersetze in folgenden Sätzen die **fett gedruckten** Satzteile:

1. I gave **Paul** the money.
2. **My mother** sent a letter to **her sister**.
3. She bought **her friends** an ice-cream.
4. **Our English teacher** gave **me and the other pupils** a test yesterday.
5. **My friends and I** sent **a postcard** to **our American friends** by airmail.
6. **My brother** gave **the dog the old sausages**.
7. **Our father** bought **those gold earrings** for **our mother** last year.
8. **Our teachers** showed **my friends and me some old photos**.
9. Can **Yvonne** lend **my sister those old jeans**?

14.3 Die *-self/-selves*-Pronomen

Mit den englischen -self/-selves-Pronomen kann man:

1. anzeigen, dass die Handlung des Verbs das Subjekt selbst betrifft. In diesem Fall sind sie Objekt im Satz und entsprechen den deutschen Reflexivpronomen (= rückbezügliche Pronomen) „mich/dich/sich, uns/euch/sich". Vergleiche:

She saw **her** in the mirror. She saw **herself** in the mirror.	Sie sah **sie** im Spiegel. Sie sah **sich** im Spiegel.
They helped **them**. They helped **themselves**.	Sie halfen **ihnen**. Sie halfen **sich**. ODER: Sie bedienten **sich**.

2. eine Person oder eine Sache besonders stark hervorheben. In dieser Funktion entsprechen sie dem deutschen „selbst". Vergleiche:

I can do it. I can do it **myself**. I don't need any help.	Ich kann es machen. Ich kann es **selbst** machen. Ich brauche keine Hilfe.

In beiden Funktionen muss die betroffene Person oder Sache in derselben grammatischen „Person" stehen:

I talked to the President **myself**.	(betont die „ich"-Form: Ich **selbst** ...)
I talked to **the President himself**.	(betont, dass ich mit dem Präsidenten selbst sprach, nicht mit seinem Stellvertreter)

Fassen wir die einzelnen Formen in einigen Beispielsätzen zusammen:

Singular:	**Plural:**
I repaired my bike **myself**.	**We** bought **ourselves** some new jeans.
Did **you** see **yourself** on TV?	**You** must read the book **yourselves**.
He copied this CD **himself**. Has **she** hurt **herself**? **It** switches **itself** off after an hour.	**They** always do their homework **themselves**.

Beachte:

- Im Plural wird *-f* zu *-ves* : *myself* → *ourselves* etc.
- Es gibt unterschiedliche Formen für *you* in Singular und Plural: *yourself* (Singular) und *yourselves* (Plural).
- Die Redewendung ***by** myself*, ***by** himself* etc. heißt „allein" oder „ohne Hilfe":

I was at the party **myself**.	Ich **selbst** war auf der Party.
I went to the party **by myself**.	Ich ging **allein** auf die Party. (= ohne Begleitung)
I made this model **all by myself**.	Ich habe dieses Modell ganz ohne Hilfe gebastelt.

Merke:

Im Gegensatz zum Deutschen hat die englische Sprache wenig echte rückbezügliche Verben (Reflexivverben). Die meisten deutschen Reflexivverben (z. B. „**sich** waschen, **sich** anziehen, **sich** treffen, **sich** langweilen" usw.) brauchen im Englischen **kein** „mich/dich/sich, uns/euch/sich".

Vergleiche:

I get up at 7 o'clock. First I wash and get dressed. Then I sit down and have breakfast. After breakfast I set off to school. My friends and I meet at the bus-stop.	Ich stehe um 7 Uhr auf. Zuerst wasche ich **mich** und ziehe **mich** an. Dann setze ich **mich** hin und frühstücke. Nach dem Frühstück mache ich **mich** auf den Weg zur Schule. Meine Freunde und ich treffen **uns** an der Bushaltestelle.

Für Englischsprachige ist es nämlich selbstverständlich, dass man sich selbst wäscht, anzieht usw. und nicht jemand anders. Wäre jemand anders gemeint, würde man die Person als Objekt erwähnen müssen: *I wash **my little brother** and dress **my baby sister**.*

6

Setze das richtige Pronomen in folgende Sätze ein. Aber Vorsicht! Es handelt sich nicht immer um eines der *-self/-selves*-Pronomen.

1. "I always do my homework ________________. Nobody helps ________________."
   "What about your sister? Does ________________ do her homework ________________?" "Well, she's younger than me. Sometimes my father helps ________________."
2. Some of the girls in my class make their clothes ________________. I've tried making my own clothes, but when I put them on and look at ________________ in a mirror, I hope that other people won't laugh at ________________ when they see ________________!
3. "I'm thirsty," he asked me. "Can I get ________________ a glass of orange juice?"
   "Of course!" I said. "Help ________________!" So he poured ________________ a glass of orange juice. "Shall I pour a glass for ________________?" he asked me and my brother. "No, thanks," I said. "We can pour ________________ a glass when we're thirsty."
4. We have a big garden, so we grow a lot of our own food ________________. Our neighbours have tried growing their food ________________, but they only have a small garden.
5. My cat is very clever. When it's hungry, it goes into the kitchen and gets ________________ something to eat. The box of cat food is on the floor. The cat knocks ________________ over. Some bits of food fall out of it, and the cat eats ________________.

7

Was würdest du in folgenden Sätzen besonders betonen? Subjekt oder Objekt?

"I was in London last week." – "We were in London ____________________. We didn't see you there." – "Well, London ____________________ is a big city, isn't it? I went on a tour of Buckingham Palace. It was a very expensive tour, so we had to pay for our tickets ____________________. Prince Charles ____________________ was the tour guide! The rooms ____________________ were very interesting,but I wanted to see the Queen ____________________.There was a door with a sign 'NO ENTRY'. When nobody was looking, I opened the door and walked right into the private rooms of the Royal Family ____________________! They ____________________ live right in the middle of the Palace ____________________. There was nobody about, so I had to find the Queen's living-room ____________________. At last I found it – and there was Her Majesty ____________________, sitting in an armchair and reading a newspaper." – "I don't believe you! You made that story up ____________________!" – "You're right. But both of you almost believed my story ____________________, didn't you?"

14.4 Die „reziproken" Pronomen *each other / one another*

Die reziproken Pronomen *each other* und *one another* drücken aus, dass zwischen Personen eine wechselseitige Beziehung besteht:

> Paul and Anna started fighting and hurt **each other / one another**.
> (= Paul hurt Anna and Anna hurt Paul.)
> *Paul und Anna fingen an, sich zu raufen und verletzten* ***sich (gegenseitig)***.

Die beiden reziproken Pronomen *each other* und *one another* sind gleichbedeutend und können beliebig eingesetzt werden.

Achtung:
Verwechsle nicht die reziproken (= wechselseitigen) Pronomen *each other / one another* mit den reflexiven (= rückbezüglichen) *-self/-selves*-Pronomen:

> Paul and Anna fell off their skateboards and hurt **themselves**.
> (= Paul hurt **him**self and Anna hurt **her**self.)
> *Paul und Anna fielen von ihren Skateboards und verletzten* ***sich***.

8

Ergänze folgende Sätze entweder mit *each other / one another* oder mit einem der *-self/-selves*-Pronomen.

1. "Hi, Karen. Have you met my brother Vincent?" – "Oh yes. Vincent and I have known ______________________ for years."
2. Some of my friends are not very good at English. So we sometimes meet after school and help ______________________ with our homework.
3. A farmer in our village had too many apples last year. He put a lot of apples in a box beside the road with a sign on it: FREE APPLES. HELP ______________________. So we helped ______________________ ____________.

4. She was too big for her old bike, so she bought ____________________ a new one.
5. I hadn't seen my cousin for six years. When we met again last week, we hardly recognized ____________________.
6. We went to the open-air concert in the afternoon and watched it again on TV in the evening. We saw ____________________ in the crowd.
7. "They never think about other people. They are selfish. They only think about ____________________." – "I hate selfish people! I think everybody should help ____________________."
8. "I painted that picture of the river ____________________. Do you like it?" – "The picture ____________________ is OK, but I don't like the colours much!"
9. "I grew up in London. Have you ever been to London ______________?" – "No. Only to London Airport, not to London ______________."
10. Nobody can help us. We'll have to do it ____________________.
11. "Shall I tell Mum and Dad that I broke your window, Mrs Smith?" – "No, John. I'll tell your parents ____________________."
12. "Did I see you and Vera talking to ____________________ at the party?" – "That's right. She didn't know many people ______________. In fact she told me she had come to the party by ______________."

14.5 Die Possessivpronomen

Neben den Possessivbegleitern *my, your, his, her* usw., die vor einem Substantiv stehen, gibt es einige Possessivpronomen, die (ähnlich wie Personalpronomen) ein Wiederholen des Substantivs vermeiden.

Singular:

Personalpronomen	Possessivbegleiter + Nomen	Possessivpronomen
I	"This isn't **my English book**."	– "No, it's **mine**." (meins)
you	"Can I borrow **your book**?"	– "No. Look for **yours** first!" (deins)
he	"I think this is **his CD**."	– "Are you sure it's **his**? It could be **mine**."
she	"Isn't that **her bike**?"	– "No. I don't think it's **hers**. It looks like **Vera's**."
it	The dog is sleeping on **its** bed.	(keine Entsprechung für *its* !)

Plural:

Personalpronomen	Possessivbegleiter + Nomen	Possessivpronomen
we	"**Our** English teacher is very good."	– "Yes. He's better than **ours**!"
you	"Can we borrow **your bikes**?"	– "What have you done with **yours**?"
they	"Have you seen **their new car**?"	– "No." – "That's **theirs** over there."

Bei Eigennamen oder Nomen im Genitiv wird einfach die Genitivform als Pronomen übernommen:

"Is that **John's skateboard**?" – "No. I think it's **Andy's**."
"I like **your sister's bike**!" – "That's **my mother's**."
"Is that **the Smiths' house**?" – "No. It's **the Browns'**."

Bei mehreren Personennamen ist nur ein Genitiv-s erforderlich:
We stayed for a week at **Chris and Geoff's**.

Achtung: Diese Pronomen bzw. Genitivformen werden in der Wendung „ein Freund **von mir**, ein Fehler **von dir**" usw. benutzt:
He's a friend **of mine**.
(= He's one of my friends – *einer unter mehreren*)

9

Setze die richtigen Possessivpronomen in folgende Dialoge ein:

1. "Whose bike is that? Is it ____________?" – "No, it isn't ____________. I didn't bring ____________ to school today. Ask Peter – I think it's ________."
2. (After the party) "Where did you put your coats?" – "We put ____________ on the bed. I think Barbara and Ken put ____________ on the bed, too."
3. "Have you seen my English books, Sheila?" – "No, Helen. These are my books. Where did you leave ____________?" – "I left them here, on the table, right next to ____________." – "Oh dear! Tania thought those books were ____________. She put them in her bag and went home, I think." – "Just a minute, Sheila. There's a bag over there. I think it's ____________. She must still be here. I'll find her and ask her about the books."

10

Ergänze die Sätze mit der richtigen Form der in Klammern stehenden Namen oder Substantive. Es sind aber auch einige Lücken **ohne** Vorgaben, die du mit den passenden Pronomen ausfüllen musst.

Beispiel: "Does this computer belong to you?" – **(my sister)** –
"No, it's *my sister's*."

1. "That must be Mr Jones's car over there." – **(Mr Smith)**
   "No. I think it's ____________________________."
2. "It wasn't my mistake. **(our headmaster)**
   It was ____________________________: he ordered the wrong books."
3. "Is that your house?" – **(the Browns)** "No, that's ____________________________.
   ____________________________ is next door."
4. "Are those your glasses?" – "No, I'm wearing ____________________________.
   (Mum) They must be ____________________________."
5. "Do you know Alice and Paul Smith?" – **(us)**
   "Of course. They're good friends of ____________________________."

Die Pronomen

Hier hast du eine Zusammenfassung aller wichtigen Pronomen und der dazugehörigen Possessivbegleiter:

Objektpronomen	Subjektpronomen	Possessivbegleiter	Reflexivpronomen	Possessivpronomen
You know **me**!	**I** bake	**my** cakes	**myself**.	**Mine** always taste best!
I don't believe **you**!	**You** did	**your** homework	**yourself**?	**Yours** got the best mark.
Do you know **him**?	**He** repairs	**his** old car	**himself**.	**His** is that car over there.
I don't like **her**.	**She** loves	**her** Jaguar and	**herself**.	**Hers** must be a lonely life!
I've never seen **it**.	**It** sits in	**its** garage all by	**itself**.	***She** never drives it.
You really mean **us**?	**We** grow	**our** own food for	**ourselves**.	**Ours** is not for sale!
I don't trust **them**!	**They** help	**their** friends and	**themselves**.	**Theirs** is a selfish attitude.
				*Es gibt kein Possessivpronomen zu *it*.

Im Gegensatz zum Deutschen

1. gibt es keine unterschiedlichen Formen für das direkte und das indirekte Objektpronomen: *When she saw **me** she gave **me** the money.* – Als sie **mich** sah, gab sie **mir** das Geld.
2. gibt es im Englischen eindeutige Pronomen für das mehrdeutige „sie/Sie"-Pronomen im Deutschen:
   sie lebt = ***she** lives*, Sie leben = ***you** live*, sie leben = ***they** live*
3. wird im Englischen kein Unterschied zwischen „sich" usw. (Reflexivpronomen) und „selbst" gemacht – in beiden Fällen benutzt man die *-self/-selves-Pronomen*:
   She saw **herself** in the mirror. — Sie sah **sich** im Spiegel.
   She did it **herself**. — Sie tat es **selbst**.
4. wird im Englischen eindeutig zwischen „sich" usw. als Reflexivpronomen und „sich" usw. als reziprokes Pronomen unterschieden:

Reflexivpronomen:
They fell off their skateboards and injured **themselves**. — Sie stürzten von ihren Skateboards und verletzten **sich**.

reziprokes Pronomen:
The skateboarders collided and injured **each other / one another**. — Die Skateboardfahrer stießen zusammen und verletzten **sich**.

Setze die richtigen Pronomen in folgenden Dialog ein. In einem Fall brauchst du auch die Präposition *to* vor dem Pronomen – aber nur in einem!

The twins (Zwillinge) Kenneth and Victor are arguing – as usual. Their mother comes in to see what is going on.

1. *Mum:* Victor? Kenneth? What's all that shouting about? What are ___________ doing?
2. *Victor:* Ken's playing with my game-boy! Give it ___________ back!
3. *Kenneth:* It's not your game-boy, Vic. It's ___________!

   Mum: So whose game-boy is this one under the table?
4. *Kenneth:* Oh! Sorry, Vic. This one belongs ___________. I must have dropped it …

   Mum: Anyway, didn't you two want to go surfing on the Internet this afternoon with Chris and Bonzo?
5. *Kenneth:* No, they're no friends of ___________!

   Mum: Well, I saw their mother at the supermarket this morning. She said you two had invited them to come round here after school to try out your new computer.

   Victor: Are you sure it was Chris and Bonzo's mother? Mrs Brown from Number 193?
6. *Mum:* Of course I'm sure. I spoke to her ___________.
7. *Kenneth:* We didn't invite them, Mum. They must have invited ______________________!
8. *Mum:* What's wrong? Don't you like them? I thought all the boys and girls in your class liked ______________________.
9. *Victor:* Most of us do, Mum, and Bonzo ________________ is OK. But nobody likes Chris Brown much.

Lösungen

1 *Simple present* oder *present progressive*?

1

Present simple forms:
I **live** in Carlisle.
My family **live** in a small house (near the town centre).
My mother **works** at a supermarket.
I **go** to the local comprehensive school and my sister **goes** to the junior school next door.
What kind of sports **do** you **like**?
I **hate** it/my name and everyone **calls** me Pat.
I **don't know** your name.
Our teacher **says** she will send all our letters in one envelope.
I **hope** that your letter is a bit longer than mine!
Tell me where you **live**, what you **do** in your free time (and something about your family).
Auxiliary verbs:
My name **is** Pat.
Carlisle **is** a town (on the border between England and Scotland).
It**'s** near the sea.
My father **is** a bus-driver.
He **hasn't** got a job.
There **is** a lot of unemployment … and it **is** difficult to find work.
My hobbies **are** skateboarding, swimming, football and playing computer games.
My full name **is** Patricia.
This **is** my first letter to you.
I hope that your letter **is** a bit longer than mine!

2

Lösungsvorschläge:
My Uncle Jürgen/Aunt Melanie lives in Bochum.
My Uncle Jürgen and my Aunt Melanie live in Bochum.
I go to school in Neuenstadt. My brother/sister goes to school in Neuenstadt.
My brothers/sisters/brothers and sisters go to school in Neuenstadt.
My mother/father works at a bank/factory/an office.
My best friend lives in Nürnberg/a small village near me.
Some of my friends go to school in Stuttgart/work at the weekends/live in Berlin.

3

1. Do you ever go to London? - We often go to London Airport to see the planes. And what about you? - We go shopping there every week.
2. We never buy "The Sun". But "The Times" is always very interesting.
3. I rarely have time to read a daily newspaper, but I sometimes buy a weekly paper.
4. Do you go to a disco regularly at the weekend? - I seldom have time - especially at the weekend. At the weekend I often go to the cinema.
5. Does she walk to school every day? - No, I often see her at the bus-stop. She always takes a 49 bus to town.

4

1. "My Uncle Jeff/He lives in Windsor, too." — 2. "Paul/He goes swimming every Friday, too." — 3. "They like ice-cream, too." — 4. "I/We play football on Saturdays, too." — 5. "She speaks French, too." — 6. "My mother does the cooking." — 7. She/Sheila plays the piano well, too." — 8. "Their mother flies to Spain for her holidays every year, too." — 9. "Patrick/He cleans his bike every week, too." — 10. "The dog often sits beside the fire, too."

5

a) *Simple form:*

You **mean** Christian?
He **comes** from Germany.
In the house where the Jenkins normally **live**.
I **see**.
Does Christian **speak** good English?
He only **speaks** German at home.
Hardly anyone at our school **learns** German.
Don't you **like** French?
Christian **says** that English is easier (for him than Russian).
Why **don't** you **come** to the youth club this evening?

Progressive form:

His father **is working** over here in England (for a year).
So where **is** the family **living** now?
Mr Jenkins **is working** in Germany (for a year).
He and his family **are living** in the Meiers' flat/in Dresden.
We**'re learning** German at our school.

b) Die einfache Präsensform wird häufig für Handlungen benutzt, die nicht im Augenblick stattfinden. Die Verlaufsform wird für Handlungen benutzt, die im Augenblick passieren oder (beim Satz *We're learning German at our school*) in einem größeren gegenwärtigen Zeitpunkt ablaufen, der als vorübergehend empfunden wird.

6

1. The boys are playing football. — 2. The girl is (tele)phoning/ringing (a friend). — 3. The woman is driving to Oxford. — 4. The man is cooking (something/lunch) (in the kitchen). — 5. The/Two/The two girls are playing table-tennis. — 6. The cat is drinking milk. — 7. The book is lying on the table. — 8. The men are (going) shopping/doing the shopping. — 9. The teacher is teaching English/giving an English lesson/standing in front of the blackboard.

7

1. Now Sylvia is doing her homework. - Sometimes Sylvia does her homework in the garden.
2. We never smoke cigarettes. - We are smoking now.
3. Do you speak English often? - Are you speaking English now?
4. He doesn't sit there every day. - He isn't sitting there now.
5. They are cycling to school this week. - They cycle to school every morning.

8

1. They aren't/are not German. — 2. Where do you live? — 3. They don't/do not like icecream. — 4. His sister Sheila doesn't/does not read comics. — 5. Who is he writing to? - - 6. He doesn't/does not (often) write postcards. — 7. Has she got a bike? — 8. We can't/cannot speak Welsh. — 9. Where does your sister work? — 10. How much do those CDs cost? — 11. Which bus are they waiting for? — 12. What's/What is he doing there?

9

1. is buying — 2. goes — 3. give — 4. like — 5. gets/comes/arrives — 6. phone — 7. go swimming — 8. What time do you usually get/come/arrive back

Test

1. **I'm learning** English at the moment.
2. She **rarely goes** swimming.
3. My father **owns** a big car now.
4. **Does** John **live** in Stuttgart?
5. My friend Peter **comes** to my house every week.
6. He **does** not know the answer.
7. Where **are** you going now?
8. I **don't** like ice-cream.
9. On Mondays I **always arrive** late at school.
10. **Do** you **like** potatoes with your meat?

Simple past oder *past progressive*? 2

1

Lösungsvorschläge:

a) I got up at 7 o'clock, had a shower/got washed, got dressed and had breakfast (in the kitchen). I left the house at 7.30 and walked to school. When I arrived at school I talked to my friends. We had English/PE/German and played (football) in the playground (during the break). Then we wrote a test. I went home at 12.30 a.m./1.00 p.m. and I had lunch. Then I did my homework and watched TV/a video/listened to my CDs/music on the radio. I went to bed at 9.45 p.m.

b) While I was having a shower/getting washed, I listened to the news on the radio.
While I was having breakfast (in the kitchen), the doorbell/phone rang.
While I was walking to school, I saw our English teacher on his bike.
While I was talking to my friends in the playground, the bell went for the first lesson.
While we were having English/PE/German, the school caught fire.
While we were playing (football) in the playground (during break), we/I/a boy/girl …
While I was going home/having lunch/doing my homework/watching TV/a video/listening to my CDs/music on the radio, I heard/saw …

2

1. saw, was waiting — 2. was getting, fell — 3. ran, was still lying — 4. was, was examining — 5. was leaving, sat — 6. was baking, went — 7. was looking, came — 8. had to, were waiting — 9. was, was giving — 10. was putting, rang — 11. went, were standing

3

1. was, arrived — 2. was raining, was blowing — 3. remembered, did not have — 4. went, phoned — 5. was getting, rang — 6. heard, got — 7. took, wrapped — 8. wanted, rang — 9. dropped, walked — 10. was just going, heard — 11. ran, turned — 12. opened, was standing — 13. told, was coming — 14. was, rang — 15. walked, picked — 16. was

4

While Tania and her Uncle Jonathan **were** having breakfast, Jethro **arrived**. Jethro **worked** on Uncle Jonathan's farm. Jethro **sat** down at the table and Uncle Jonathan **gave** him a cup of tea. Aunt Helen **came** into the kitchen while they **were drinking** their tea. "Good morning, Jethro," she **said**. "I **saw** you in the village yesterday. You **were talking** to Joe Smith the policeman. What **did** he **want** to talk to you about?" "I'm afraid I can't tell you, Mrs Brown," Jethro **answered**. "It's a secret."

5

1. During — 2. While — 3. while — 4. during — 5. While — 6. during — 7. During — 8. While

6

1. During our drive through the forest we saw several bears.
2. While he was walking across the park, he got very wet.
3. I went to Bristol during my stay in England last summer.
4. She phoned her boyfriend while she was having her lunch break.
5. During our performance of "Hamlet" there was a fire in the school hall.
6. While we were flying to New York, the weather got worse.
7. The fans screamed all the time while the Rolling Stones were playing at their concert.
8. We stopped five times while we were driving to Scotland.
9. During his exams he lost about two kilos.

7

Bei den Lösungen dieser Aufgabe bieten wir die Sätze in der für Engländer natürlichsten Kombination von Haupt- und Nebensatz an. Normalerweise ist die Reihenfolge dann: *while + was + -ing* am Anfang, *when + past simple* an zweiter Stelle. In den meisten Fällen kann die umgekehrte Reihenfolge auch als richtig gelten.

1. While the boys were playing football, it began to rain.
2. The girl was having a bath when the telephone rang.
3. While the woman was waiting for the bus, she read/was reading the (news) paper.
4. The girl was washing her hair when her friend arrived.
5. While the (two) boys were playing cards, the teacher entered the room.
6. The sun was setting when we arrived at the hotel.
7. While the boy was washing up, the girls were watching/watched TV.
8. When the bus arrived, the girl got on.
9. While the postman was delivering the/our letters, a/our dog attacked/bit him.

Test

Sunday **was** Aunt Helen's birthday. On Saturday evenings, Aunt Helen and Uncle Jonathan usually **visited** friends. Tania stayed at home that Saturday evening and watched TV. She was hungry, so she made herself a couple of sandwiches **during** one of the breaks. **While** she was watching a film, the doorbell **rang**. She was alone in the farmhouse, so she **looked** out of the window before she opened the door. Joe Smith the policeman was standing outside! When she **saw** that Jethro and five or six other people were with him, she thought that something must be wrong! She opened the door. "Don't worry," said Jethro **when** he saw her anxious face. "This is our surprise for your Aunt Helen Your aunt told me that she and your uncle **were visiting** Mr and Mrs Jenkins down in the village tonight. So we **decided** to have a little party with a few more friends. After all, they won't be back until nearly midnight – and your aunt's birthday starts then!"

3 *Simple past* oder *present perfect*?

1

[1]W	E	[2]R	E		[3]L			[4]S	H	O	O	[5]K		
A		A		[6]B	I	T		P				N		[7]C
[8]S	[9]A	N	[10]G		T		[11]F	E	L	L		E		A
	T		O					L			[12]S	W	A	M
[13]W	E	N	T		[14]C			[15]T	O	R	E			E
O				S	H	O	[17]T				N		[18]B	
[19]R	O	[20]S	E		O		H		[21]S	A	T		R	
E		A			[22]S	T	O	L	E				O	
		[23]W	O	[24]K	E		U		T		[25]S	H	U	T
				E			G				L		G	
	[26]S	W	E	P	T		[27]H	I	D		E		H	
				T			T				[28]P	U	T	
[29]F	E	L	T					[30]L	O	S	T			

2

1. got — 2. took — 3. went — 4. ran — 5. were — 6. drove — 7. saw — 8. spoke — 9. knew — 10. stood

3

a) *Present perfect:*

I **haven't seen** him for days. — He **hasn't been** at the pub since last Saturday. — He**'s been** away all week. — He's the only person who has suddenly **disappeared**. — But **I've known** Andy for thirty years! — He**'s** never **stolen** anything! — Have you **phoned** his sister in London yet? — Maybe he**'s gone** to visit her.

Simple past:

Did you **see** Andy Wilson (at the pub) last night? — **Was** he at the pub last night? What **did** you **want** to see him about? — Someone **stole** three or four sheep (from Farmer Hunt's field one night last week). — What makes you think that Andy **stole** them? — We **found** two of the sheep in his barn yesterday. — That doesn't mean he **stole** them! — I **didn't know** he **had** a sister in London. — … if I **were** you

b) Andy Wilson has never stolen anything in his life.
Andy Wilson hasn't been to the pub since Saturday.
Andy Wilson wasn't at the pub last night.
Jethro has known Andy for years.
Jethro hasn't seen Andy for some days.
Joe Smith didn't know about Andy's sister.
Joe Smith hasn't phoned Andy's sister yet.
Someone stole some sheep last week.

4

a) 1. "Have you seen John this morning?" — 2. "No, but I have just arrived. — 3. Perhaps he has already gone to his classroom." — 4. "No. I have already looked in his classroom. There's nobody there."

b) 5. "How's your sister Stella? She hasn't been to the youth club for a few weeks." — 6. "Didn't you know? She has flown to the USA for a year. — 7. She has got a job as an au-pair girl." — 8. "Lucky Stella! Has she written a letter home yet?" — 9. "No, she hasn't had time. She only left yesterday. — 10. But she has promised to phone as soon as she can."

(Kurzformen sind selbstverständlich auch erlaubt.)

5

1. I just hope you know what you're doing! — 2. He just shouted at me. He wouldn't listen. — 3. She has just gone. If you run, you'll catch her up. — 4. They just didn't listen to their friends' advice. — 5. We just thought you might want to come with us. — 6. I have just seen a ghost. — 7. They have just sold their house. — 8. We have just received a letter from Stella.

6

1. did you do/were you doing — 2. watched/was watching — 3. was — 4. have seen — 5. Did you watch — 6. didn't/did not have — 7. have been — 8. saw — 9. showed — 10. Have you ever seen — 11. went — 12. have misunderstood — 13. didn't mean; meant — 14. saw — 15. Have you ever seen

7

1. Have you ever kept sheep in your barn? — 2. Did you see (the) sheep in Farmer Hunt's field last week? — 3. Have you ever been to London? — 4. When was your first visit to London? — 5. Did you stay with your sister? — 6. How long has your sister lived in London? — 7. When did you go back to your farm? — 8. Did you find any sheep in your/the barn? — 9. Did you phone the police? — 10. Why didn't you phone the police?

8

Johnny Purple was born in 1980. From 1980 to 1997 he lived in London. From 1986 to 1996 he went to/attended Croydon Comprehensive School. From 1996 to 1997 he worked as an assistant in a music shop; he took guitar lessons for 2 years. From 1998 until/to now he has been a singer in the pop group "Johnny's Purple Hearts". He/The group has made six singles and one CD so far. He/The group has been on three tours to Europe and America. He/They went on a tour to South Africa last year./He/They toured South Africa last year. He married Sally Johnson in 2004. He got a divorce/ They were divorced one year later.

Test

1. "**Have** you **done** your homework yet?"
2. "Yes, Mum. I **did** it when I got home from school."
3. "That's what you **told** me yesterday!"
4. "It was true! You just **did**n't **believe** me!"
5. "Are you sure you **finished** everything before you put the TV on?"
6. "Yes, Mum. **Has** Dad **come** home from work?"
7. "Yes. He **has** just **arrived**. Why?"
8. "Well, a few days ago he **said** he would test my French vocabulary with me.
9. We **have**n't **had** a French vocabulary test for about a month, but we've got one tomorrow."
10. "**Did**n't your class **have** a vocabulary test on Monday?" "Yes, Mum. But that was for German. French is tomorrow."

Simple present perfect oder *present perfect progressive*? 4

1

1. have you been learning — 2. has been living — 3. haven't been standing — 4. has your brother been working — 5. Has Julie been playing — 6. have been listening — 7. has been lying — 8. have you been doing — 9. have been watching — 10. have we been waiting — 11. have been eating — 12. has been drinking

2

1. "What have you been doing all afternoon?" - "I've been working in the garden."
2. "Have you done your homework yet?" - "Yes, I have just finished it."
3. "Have you written to your uncle?" - "Yes, but I haven't posted the letter yet."
4. "Who has been using my pen? I can't find it." - "I haven't seen it anywhere."
5. "Where have you been? I've been looking for you all morning!"
6. "All the lights have just gone out. What have you been doing?" -
7. "I haven't been doing anything. John and I have been sitting in the kitchen all evening."
8. "You've got chocolate around your mouth. Have you been eating my chocolates again?" - "Me? No - I haven't eaten anything since lunch."
9. "Look at these cigarette ends on the ground under the window! Someone has been standing here for a long time in the dark and has been watching us through the window!"
10. "I have often stood here waiting for a bus." - "Have you ever thought of taking a taxi?"

3

1. Melanie 2. Vincent 3. Jerry 4. Paul 5. Claire

4

"I was born in London 16 years ago but I have lived in Birmingham since my parents moved there in 1986. My father worked as a clerk for 15 years but he had to give up his office job five years ago and has been a postman since 2001. My mother has worked in a kindergarten since I started grammar school five years ago. I have one brother aged 18 and a younger sister aged 12. I am looking for a job now. Since May I have written to several firms. I wrote to your firm some weeks ago but …"

5

A	L	O	S	T	Z	B	F	B	S
S	W	P	P	Q	S	E	E	N	P
K	U	W	O	N	A	G	A	E	E
G	T	A	K	E	N	U	T	R	N
N	I	K	E	T	D	N	E	T	T
G	O	V	N	W	G	O	N	E	N
D	R	I	E	E	N	N	N	S	Y
G	A	S	P	N	N	T	S	E	M

1. lost
2. spoken
3. taken
4. seen
5. eaten
6. gone
7. been
8. begun
9. done
10. won
11. given
12. spent

Test

"Where have you been? I have been waiting for you for half an hour!"
"Sorry I'm late. I waited over twenty minutes for a bus. But in the end I walked here. Let me sit down. I'm so tired! I feel as if I have been walking all afternoon!"
"Never mind. Sit down. If you walked all the way you have deserved a rest!"
"Where's Geoff? Hasn't he arrived yet?" "He has just sent me an SMS. He's standing outside the wrong disco! He's been there since seven o'clock. I sent him an SMS back. He'll be here in a few minutes."

5 Das *past perfect*

1

My boyfriend Geoff had read about it in a computer magazine.
After we had waited for about a quarter of an hour, Peter got out again.
The porter … told us that the train to Birmingham had left ten minutes ago.
Geoff told the porter that the man at the ticket office had said "Platform 1".
The porter said the man had meant "the front end of Platform 1".
We had got into the last coach.
The train to Birmingham had been the first four coaches … They had already gone, and we had been in one of the last four coaches which had been (= *Passiv*) left behind.

2

1. After they had checked their equipment, they packed their clothes.
2. After they had packed their clothes, they cycled to the Lake District.
3. After they had cycled to/arrived in the Lake District, they found a camping site.

4. After they had found a camping site, they went shopping (in the village).
5. After they had gone/been shopping (in the village), they made and ate supper.
6. After they had made and eaten supper, they went to bed.

3

1. After/Because we had bought tickets, we went to the pop concert.
2. a) After they had sold their house, they bought a bungalow.
2. b) They sold their house after/because they had bought a bungalow.
3. I phoned the police after/because my car had been stolen.
4. a) After she had left school, she found a job.
4. b) She left school because/after she had found a job.
5. Did you go to Brighton after you had visited London?
6. Because I had phoned the number quickly I got the job.
7. The old woman shouted at the girl because she had burned the cakes.
8. After we had found out their address, we wrote them a letter.
9. He phoned his parents after he had arrived in England.
10. After/Because I had passed my driving test, I bought a motor-bike.
11. I went to the lost-property office because/after I had lost my umbrella.
12. a) After they had lost the match, they drank a lot of beer.
12. b) They lost the match after/because they had drunk a lot of beer.
13. We had come to London because we wanted to improve our English.
14. a) She went swimming after/because she had bought a new bikini.
14. b) After she had gone swimming, she bought a new bikini.
15. After the tourists had visited the castle, they went back to their hotel.

4

1. We looked at the scenery after the train had left the station.
2. After we had passed Rugby Station, the train went into a long tunnel.
3. Suddenly the train stopped before we had reached the end of the tunnel.
4. After the train had stopped, the guard came into our coach.
5. He wanted to know if anyone had pulled the emergency brake.
6. Nobody said anything because nobody had pulled the emergency brake.
7. Some passengers were frightened because the train had stopped in a/the tunnel.
8. After the guard had told the passengers that there was no need to worry, he spoke to the driver on/over the train telephone.
9. Before the guard had finished speaking, we heard the driver's voice over the coach loudspeakers.
10. He told us that there had been a small fault in the train's computer system but that everything was OK now.
11. Five minutes later the train started to move again.

5

"How long **had** you **been living** here before you moved to London?" - "Three years." — 2. He started to learn French after he **had been studying** English for two years. — 3. People **had been drinking** 'Wonder-Cola' for years before scientists discovered that it was a serious danger to health.— 4. The bus only arrived after the passengers **had been waiting** in the rain for almost an hour. — 5. She became the boss's assistant before she **had been working** at the firm for six months. — 6 "You looked very dirty when I saw you yesterday! What **had** you **been doing**?" — 7. "I **had been digging** the garden." — 8. The pop group **had not been playing** long when the fire started. — 9. "How long **had** she **been smoking** cigarettes before her doctor told her to stop?" - "Only about two years."

6

1. had been writing; had not written — 2. had been collecting; had now collected — 3. had never travelled; had been travelling — 4. had you been driving; had driven

FOOTBALL IN THE PARK:
5. had been playing; had always played — 6. had been working — 7. had ever seen — 8. had been watching — 9. had been talking

Test

1. After I **had** finished my homework, I watched TV.
2. I **had been learning** English for two years before I **went** to Britain for the first time.
3. She **had finished** her lunch long before I **arrived**.
4. My father **had been driving** for half an hour when he realized that he was on the wrong road.
5. He told me that he **had borrowed** my book.
6. After he **had gone** home I saw that he **had forgotten** to take his CDs with him.
7. When he **(had) arrived** I told him that he **was** late.
8. I **went** out to play football with them after I had finished my homework.
9. Before I **got** up I **had** already **had** breakfast - in bed!
10. We **(had) walked** to the station before the rain began, so we didn't get wet.

Will-future, going to-future und *present progressive*

6

1

Neutrale Zukunft mit *will/won't* :
(I expect) we'll go to the seaside again. — Won't you need a lot of special equipment? — We won't take more than we need this time! — … 20 kilos will have to be enough. — … so I'll ask him. — I'll phone you when I've seen him. Will you be at home at about 6? — We'll see each other at the youth club. — I'll see you there at about half past six.

Verlaufsform der Gegenwart mit Zeitangabe:
John and I are going camping in Turkey this year. — Is John coming to the youth club tonight? — I'm seeing him after school. — I'm not going to my jazz gymnastics tonight.

Absicht mit *going to* :
What are you going to do this summer, Claire? — We're going to fly to Istanbul. — I'm going to bring Barbara with me. — Barbara is going to come anyway.

2

1. People will (be able to) use language translation telephones. We/They won't have to learn (foreign) languages any more.
2. Pupils/Children won't go to school. They will use home computers. We/They will listen to our/their lessons and see them on the computer screen.
3. People won't have to work. Robots will do everything.
4. We will have electric walkways. We won't (need to) take the bus or walk to school. There will be no pollution.
5. Secretaries won't (need to) write letters and faxes by hand any more. They will only (need to) speak into typing machines.

3

Example: I'm going to walk — 1. I'm going to cycle — 2. I'm going to visit — 3. I'm going to cycle — 4. I'm going to stay — 5. I'm going to climb — 6. I'm going to pay a visit to — 7. I'm not going to spend — 8. are going to take — 9. are going to follow — 10. I'm going to catch

4

…

S: Oh, hello, Mr Wilson. Just let me look at my calendar. On Monday I'm flying to Berlin. What about Tuesday?

W: Let me see – No, on Tuesday I'm going to the computer exhibition in London, but I'll be free on Wednesday.

S: On Wednesday I'm visiting our factory in Bremen. What about Thursday?

W: Just a minute – I'm not doing anything on Thursday afternoon. …

W: Sorry. I'm playing golf with a Japanese customer. Can't we make it the afternoon?

S: No. I'm discussing a new project with my staff on Thursday afternoon. What about Friday?

W: Friday? Well I'm driving to Manchester in the morning and I'm meeting Dr Müller in Leeds in the afternoon. What are you doing on Monday next week?

5

1. The weather tomorrow will be sunny and very hot. — 2. They are cycling/going to cycle to Brighton on Thursday. — 3. The boy is going to invite the girl to his party. — 4. "Will someone answer the phone?" — 5. "I am not going to visit Spain again." — 6. Flight BE 782 will arrive at 12.15.

Test

Die Verbformen in Klammern sind auch richtige Lösungen.

1. "Bye, Paul! I'll see you at the disco tomorrow!"
2. "I won't be at the disco, Jenny.
3. I'm going (to go) to the cinema tomorrow.
4. Will you come with me?"
5. "I'll have to ask my mother.
6. How much will my ticket cost?"
7. "Nothing I'll buy (I'm going to buy) your ticket You paid last time"
8. "Fine! I'll ask Mum as soon as I get home.
9. When will you be (When are you going to be) at home this evening?"
10. "I'm going (to go) swimming this evening, but I should be back at about 9. You can ring me then."

Bedingungssätze

1

Nebensatz mit *if*	Hauptsatz
"If you turn round,	I'll shoot!"
"If you tell me where the (King of Scotland's) diamonds are,	I will let you go."
if I don't tell you where they are?"	„What will you do

Man erkennt an den Zeitformen, dass die Sprecher die Bedingungen als leicht erfüllbar ansehen: Die Zeitform *simple present* wird im *if*-Teil benutzt, die Zukunftsform mit *will* im Hauptsatz.

2

2. If I save/she saves enough money, I'll/she'll buy a dog.
3. If I work/he works hard at school, I'll/he'll go to university.
4. If I go/she goes to the party, I'll/she'll meet John.
5. If I get/he gets a well-paid job soon, I'll/he'll go to Spain for my/his holidays.
6. If my/her parents allow it, I'll/she'll invite some friends to a party.

Natürlich kann die Reihenfolge der Satzhälften umgekehrt sein.

3

1. If I learn a lot at grade school, I will/I'll go to high school.
2. If I go to high school, I will/I'll learn a lot more.
3. If I work hard, I will/I'll pass my exams.
4. If I get good marks in my exams, I will/I'll get a place at college.
5. If I go to college, I will/I'll study hard.
6. If I study very hard, I will/I'll do well at college.
7. If I pass my college exams, I will/I'll get a good job.
8. If I get a good job, I will/I'll earn a lot of money.
9. If I save some of my money, I will/I'll soon be rich.
10. If I am rich, I will/I'll be able to enjoy life while I'm still young.

4

1. when — 2. if — 3. when — 4. When — 5. If — 6. when — 7. if — 8. If — 9. if — 10. when

5

Typ II – *if + simple past:*

"If I **knew** where the diamonds/they were, I **wouldn't be** here. I'**d be** on the Bahamas ..." — "If I **had** the (King of Scotland's) diamonds, I'**d be** a multi-millionaire!" — "If you **found** the diamonds, you **would keep** them all for yourself!"

Typ I – *if + simple present:*

"Unless you **tell** me where they are, I **will shoot** you!" — "I **won't be able** to tell you where I have hidden them if you **shoot** me." — "If you **take** me to the diamonds, I'**ll share** them with you!"

6

1. If I had a bicycle, I wouldn't/I'd not have to walk to the station. — 2. If I did not/didn't have to walk to the station, I would/I'd leave home later. — 3. If I left home later in the mornings, I would/I'd have more time for breakfast. — 4. If I had more time for breakfast, I would/I'd think about new inventions. — 5. If I thought hard, I would/I'd get good ideas. — 6. If I got good ideas, I would/I'd invent useful things. — 7. If I invented useful things, I would/I'd soon get rich. — 8. If I got rich, I would/I'd give up my job on the trains. — 9. If I gave up my job, I would/I'd have more time for experiments. — 10. If I had more time for experiments, I would/I'd invent even better things.

7

Typ III: *if + past perfect*

"If only the King **had hired** a real killer (instead of saving money and trying to do the job himself), I **would** probably **have taken** him to the jewels." — "But he **would have killed** you if you **had done** that!" — "If you **had been listening** *(past perfect progressive)* to me, you **would have realized** that there was never any danger for me." — "I **would** never **have taken** such a risk if you **hadn't been waiting** *(past perfect progressive)* at the hiding place." — "If you **hadn't received** my note, how **would** you **have known** where to wait?" — "If I **had received** a note, I **would have been** there to help you."

Es handelt sich ausschließlich um Bedingungssätze des Typs III.

8

1. If I had gone to high school, I would have worked hard. — 2. If I had worked hard, I would have passed my exams. — If I had gone to college, I would not have had time to invent things. — 4. If I had done well at college, I would have become a teacher. — 5. If I had become a teacher, I would never have become an inventor. — 6. If I had

not become an inventor, I would not have invented all those useful things. — 7. If I had become a teacher, I would not have had to work so hard. — 8. If I had not worked so hard, I would perhaps have been happier. — 9. If I had moved to Europe, I would have been more successful. — 10. If I had died when I was young, I would never have invented the electric light bulb.

9

1. If you hit me, I will tell Mum!
2. If I knew her address, I would write to her.
3. If he had waited, we would have taken him with us.
4. If she helps me with my homework, I will help her with hers.
5. If you knew her better, you would like her.
6. If they had asked me to help, I would have done my best.
7. If we walk this way, we'll soon be home.
8. If the sun had shone more often, we would have had a nicer holiday.
9. If the boys brought their CDs, the girls would bring theirs.
10. If we had played harder, we wouldn't have lost the match.

10

1. would tell — 2. had — 3. see — 4. had stolen — 5. will call — 6. would have bought — 7. had not told — 8. would not have left — 9. won't/will not go — 10. ask — 11. want — 12. say — 13. doesn't stop — 14. were — 15. had known

11

1.a) If you worked hard, you might/could/should pass your exams.
1.b) If you had worked hard, you might/could/should have passed your exams.
2.a) If I talked to Jenny, she might invite me to her party.
2.b) If I had talked to Jenny, she might have invited me to her party.
3.a) If I borrowed £20, I could/might buy those CDs.
3.b) If I had borrowed £20, I could/might have bought those CDs.
4.a) If he phoned his friends in Germany, he could/might get help with his German homework.
4.b) If he had phoned his friends in Germany, he could/might have got help with his German homework.
5.a) If you helped your sister, she might/should help you.
5.b) If you had helped your sister, she might/should have helped you.

Test

1. "When will you see Pat?" – "This afternoon I'll give her your message when I see her."
2. "Will you lend me £20 if I promise to pay you back on Thursday?" – "I won't lend you any more money unless you pay me back what you already owe me! If I were you, I'd find a weekend job and earn some money instead of borrowing it!"
3. "Would you come to my party if I invited you?" – "Of course. I'd love to come. I love parties! If you hadn't invited me I would have been angry with you!"
4. "I think she's OK. I saw her yesterday. She would have gone to the doctor's if she had felt ill."
5. "We could be in New York tomorrow if we went by plane." – "If I had known you wanted to fly to New York, I would have brought my passport with me and gone with you!"
6. "You must show your German test to your father when he comes home."

8 Aktiv oder Passiv?

1

Present passive:
Sometimes strange noises are heard at night, so the room is not often used. I hope you are not disturbed. — All our visitors are told the story of the rich woman.

Past passive:
The old village inn (where we spent the night) was haunted. About fifty years ago, a woman was murdered in this room. — She was found dead one morning. — We were not disturbed (during the night). — (Later) the bullet was put in a special glass box and placed on our mantlepiece.

Present perfect passive:
(A woman was murdered) in the room you have been given.

Past perfect passive:
All the other rooms had been booked. — All her money and jewels had been stolen. — The floor had not been swept for a long time. — Had the rich woman been killed by this bullet? — ... the story of the rich woman who had been killed with it.

Hilfsverb + Passivinfinitiv:
No trace of the murderer could be found. — I hoped that we would be woken by a scream (or the sound of a gun). — The heavy bed had to be moved before we could find the ring.

2

I will be phoned tomorrow morning./I am/was/will be woken every morning at 6.30.
Many tourists were stranded at airports last week.
Mount Everest was climbed in 1953.
This car is/was made at the new factory.
When the news was announced, everyone was happy.
After the band had been introduced, the concert began.
Many new hotels have been built so far this year.
She is/was/will be woken every morning at 6.30. / She will be phoned tomorrow morning.

3

1. Rubbish is often dropped in the playground. — 2. Some money was stolen from my jacket pocket. — 3. The new English teacher is not liked. — 4. Our supper was burned. — 5. The grass is cut every week. — 6. Lunch is served at 1 p.m. — 7. Their house was broken into. — 8. The speed limit is often broken. — 9. The song "Greensleeves" was written in the 12th century. — 10. Many new houses are built every year. — 11. The two young men were arrested at the airport. — 12. These old pictures are not looked at much nowadays. — 13. Is English spoken in this shop? — 14. Was your fun spoilt? — 15. You are not expected to wait. — 16. Rome was not built in a day.

4

1. He has not been seen since January. — 2. You will be met at London Airport. — 3. These souvenirs can be bought at any seaside town. — 4. After he had been arrested he was taken to the police station. — 5. This part of the country has not been explored before. — 6. Will the beauty queen be chosen on Saturday? — 7. Don't touch that wire! You would be killed if you did! — 8. Has the Yeti ever been seen? — 9. Hasn't the murder been solved yet? — 10. All the tickets for the open-air concert can't have been sold yet! — 11. The magazine can be ordered from England. — 12. The world record has not been broken yet. — 13. The missing boy was seen in Edinburgh yesterday. — 14. After the police had been called, the burglar was arrested. — 15. This work won't/will not be finished in time.

5

a) 1. Ten years ago a lot of chemicals were used on the farms. Now farming methods have been changed.
2. Ten years ago (a lot of) rubbish was put in the river. Now the river has been cleared.

3. Ten years ago many cars were parked in the village. Motor traffic has now been banned.
4. Ten years ago a lot of coal was burned. Now the houses have been converted to central heating.
5. Ten years ago a lot of pollution was caused by the factory. The factory has now been closed.
6. Ten years ago a lot of litter was dropped in streets. Now more litter bins have been provided.
7. Ten years ago the houses were/had been made dirty by air pollution. Now they/the houses have been cleaned.

b) 1. After the farming methods had been changed the fields were/the river was cleaner/less polluted, etc.
2. After the river had been cleaned (up), more fish started to live in it.
3. After motor traffic had been banned from the village, there was less air pollution/ noise/people used the local buses more.
4. After the houses had been converted to central heating, the air was cleaner/ heating the houses was easier.
5. After the factory had been closed, there was less pollution.
6. After more litter bins had been provided, the streets were cleaner/less litter was dropped in the streets.
7. After the houses had been cleaned, they looked a lot nicer.

6

1. A lot of new houses are being built in our town. — 2. Are new trees being planted in the woods? — 3. New cars are not being bought at the moment. — 4. A piano was being played at the back of the house. — 5. A lot of cars are being stolen nowadays. — 6. Was dinner being served when you arrived? — 7. My car was not being repaired. — 8. Is the roof being repaired? — 9. Was the Queen being photographed a lot? — 10. All the nice food I made is not being eaten!

7

1. is being interviewed — 2. were already being cleared — 3. was still being dug — 4. were being broken into — 5. are they being asked — 6. are being opened — 7. was just being welcomed — 8. are being changed — 9. are being paid for — 10. are being held

8

1. The English Channel was (first) swum by Captain Webb in 1875.
2. The first car was built by Gottlieb Daimler in 1885.
3. The song "Yesterday" was composed by John Lennon in 1964.
4. The Football Association Cup was won by Manchester United last year.
5. Basketball was first played by YMCA members in America.
6. The novel "1984" was written by George Orwell in 1948.
7. The first steps on the moon were taken by Neil Armstrong in 1969.

9

1. The purse was found in the school playground last week. — 2. The letter has already been posted. — 3. The old school is being demolished (by demolition experts). — 4. All the apples had been picked before I arrived. — 5. The clock he broke cannot be replaced. — 6. This letter was written by an idiot! — 7. He took a taxi to the station because his car was being repaired. — 8. The accident must be reported to the police. — 9. We have been asked to turn the music down a bit. — 10. This fine song was written by Paul Simon.

Test

1. I **have been invited** to meet the Queen.
2. Hundreds of criminals **are caught** every day.
3. The President **wasn't told / was not told** the truth about the problem.
4. You **will be given** a new job when the new factory **is opened** (when the boss opens the new factory).
5. The garden **must be tidied** up.
6. A Christmas concert **is being arranged** at our school.
7. Hundreds of things **had been stolen** from the shops before the police **were (!) called** (before someone called the police).
8. He must **have been warned** that we were coming.
9. Survivors from the plane crash **were being interviewed** when I arrived.
10. Dozens of good songs **have been written by Elton John**.

9 Der Infinitiv

1

1. My mother always makes me finish my homework before she lets me watch TV.
2. It started to rain and we were still five kilometres from the youth hostel. So our teacher made us walk faster.
3. We live in the middle of a big town, so my parents have never let me go to school by bike. They make me walk or go by bus.
4. I was ill when we had our last English test. I hope our teacher will let me take it separately. I think I'll get a good mark for it.
5. I don't like spinach much, but my mother always makes me eat it all up. She says it's good for me.
6. Big sister: "Let me borrow your new CD. I want to listen to it!" – Little sister: "I haven't listened to it myself yet! You can't make me lend it to you!"
7. "Last week our English teacher made us learn twenty-five new English words! I hope she doesn't make us learn fifty this week!"
8. "You're coat is very wet, Eric! Have you been standing out in the rain?" – "Yes, Mum. Our teachers didn't let us stay in the classrooms during break. They made us go out into the playground."

2

Da es sich um Äußerungen über deinen persönlichen Alltag handelt, müssen unsere Musterlösungen nicht unbedingt bei dir zutreffen:

1. When I get up, my mother makes me get dressed before I have breakfast.
2. Then she lets me watch TV while I'm having breakfast.
3. Then I go to school. If it's raining, I must take an umbrella/wear a raincoat/go to school by bus but I needn't take an umbrella/wear a raincoat/go to school by bus.
4. Our English teacher lets us use a dictionary *(Wörterbuch)* when we have a test, but he/she makes us work hard/learn ten new words a day.
5. During the morning break, we can go into the playground/stay in our classrooms. But we mustn't be too noisy / go outside the school gates.
6. When I/we get home from school my mum makes me do my homework /wash my hands, but then she lets me play/watch TV/visit friends.
7. Before going to bed I may play /watch TV/visit friends, but I'm not allowed to go to discos/to stay up until 10.30

3

1. We stood outside Buckingham Palace and saw the Queen arrive.
2. I didn't actually see the accident happen. I was looking in the other direction. I only heard the car's tyres scream on the wet road. When I looked round, the car had stopped and the cyclist was already getting up from the ground.
3. The tourist in the crowded market felt someone quickly put his hand into the back pocket of her jeans. He was probably trying to steal her money.
4. I heard someone shout. I looked round and saw my friend Fred.
5. We were watching a motor race on TV. We saw two cars crash.
6. My friend actually saw the bank robbery. He saw three masked men jump out of a car and run into the bank.
7. I was waiting for my bus when I suddenly heard a car bomb explode.

4

Zuerst einige „vernünftige" Sätze:
My teacher told/ordered us to work harder.
My teacher warned/told/ordered us not to copy from each other.
My teacher likes his/her pupils to work hard.

The soldier told/ordered us to stay where we were / to go away.
The soldier told/ordered us not to come any closer/not to touch anything.

The boss ordered/told them to be quiet/work harder.
The boss requested/told them not to smoke in the building.
The boss likes us/them to work at weekends.
The boss hates us/them to arrive late for work.

The postman likes/prefers/advised me/us to keep my/our dog indoors when he comes.

The ticket inspector requested/ordered me/us/passengers/them to show him/her my/ our/their ticket(s).
The ticket inspector doesn't/didn't want me/us/passengers/them to show him/her my/our/their ticket(s).

Und jetzt ein paar Nonsens-Sätze:
My teacher prefers his/her pupils not to work hard / not to do their homework.
The soldier advised/warned us not to join the army.
The boss ordered me/us/them to go home early.
The postman hates me/us/them to give him tips *(Trinkgelder)*.
The ticket inspector advised us not to travel by train again.

Es sind unzählige andere Nonsens-Sätze möglich. Sie sind ebenfalls richtig, wenn sie unseren Mustern entsprechen!

5

1. The policeman ordered us to stand back.
2. His boss warned him not to be late again.
3. Our music teacher asked us to tell our parents about the school concert.
4. The teacher told the whole class to listen carefully.
5. The stewardess asked us to sit on the other side of the plane.
6. The boss (said that he) expected his workers to work harder.
7. My mum hates me to tell lies.
8. My father wants me to put on a clean T-shirt every day.
9. Our English teacher told us he would like us to learn five new English words a day.
10. The fireman warned the people not to come too close to the fire.

6

1. "What's the best thing **to do** in this situation?" 2. "I know which way **to go**." — 3. "I can show you the best vegetables **to grow** in your garden." — 4. There were no houses for people **to live** in. — 5. "I've got nobody **to talk** to," said the old man. — 6. John was the only one **to lose** his way. — 7. Our teacher told us what **to learn** for the class test. — 8. He asked me **how to ring Germany from Britain**. — 9. *Notice:* Will the last person **to leave** the office please turn the lights off. — 10. She asked me **when to meet me**.

7

1. The first person to climb Mount Everest was Edmund Hillary.
2. The first German to win the Men's Singles at Wimbledon was Boris Becker.
3. The last person to rule the Soviet Union was Mikhail Gorbachev.
4. The only racing driver to be World Champion five times is Michael Schumacher.
5. The first woman to swim the English Channel was Gertrude Ederle.
6. The first person to walk on the moon was Neil Armstrong.

Test

1. "Good morning. I'd like **to talk** to Dr Everard, please. I must see her at once!" — 2. "**Let** me see … — 3. I think I heard her **come** in a few minutes ago. — 4. Do you have an appointment, Mr … ?" – "Gifford, Clive Gifford. It's very important. I'm a new patient, but I'm sure Dr Everard will see me. I feel very ill …" – "Mr Gifford, there are five doctors in the surgery this morning. Why do you want **to see** one particular doctor?" — 5. "A friend of mine recommended her to me. He said she was the only doctor **to understand** all about old people's problems! — 6. I **need** to see her!" — 7. "I must ask you **to sit** down for a minute. If you're so ill, you mustn't get so excited." — 8. "You can't make me **sit** down!" — 9. "You **needn't** shout, Mr Gifford. — 10. If you

want Dr Everard to treat you, please sit down and wait a moment. I'm sure she'll see you in a minute."

Das *gerund* 10

1

(Das Blaugedruckte sind die Wörter, die das jeweilige „gerund" ergänzen)
Skateboarding – skateboarding – skiing – skateboarding – windsurfing or snowboarding? – hurting yourself – injuring other people
learning to windsurf – windsurfing – swimming – climbing out of the water – standing on their boards – mastering the basic techniques – staying on your board – windsurfing on the sea – skateboarding in the city.

2

Swimming in the sea is one of my hobbies.
Walking (in the mountains/hills) is not among my interests.
Reading (books/comics) is one of my interests/hobbies.
Eating in bed/food/sweets is one of my bad habits.
Listening to good music is (not) one of my interests.
Writing letters to friends is not among my hobbies.
Working in the garden is not one of my weekend activities.
Playing in the park is one of my weekend activities.
Washing the car is not one of my weekend activities.

Drei lustige Sätze:
Swimming in bed is one of my hobbies.
Walking in the sea is not among my interests.
Swimming to good music is one of my bad habits.

3

1. Dancing (at a disco) is fun/fantastic/a waste of time.
2. Swimming (in the sea) is dangerous/a hobby of mine/wonderful.
3. Hang-gliding is fantastic/dangerous/stupid.
4. Playing football is a waste of time/fun/super.
5. Learning English is a hobby of mine/terrible!
6. Cooking is terrible/interesting/one of my hobbies.
7. Making models is not interesting for me/a wonderful hobby.
8. Writing letters to people is boring/easy/a waste of time.
9. Cycling is easy/wonderful/boring.
10. Camping (in the country) is a hobby of mine/fun/horrible.

4

Lösungsvorschläge:

1. I like swimming. — 2. I don't mind cooking. — 3. I hate working in the garden. — 4. I prefer sailing to swimming. — 5. I'm keen on riding. — 6. I'm not so keen on cycling. — 7. I love reading. — 8. I'm (not) mad about learning English.

5

a)	b)
1. No smoking.	"No smoking" means you're not allowed to smoke here.
2. No camping.	"No camping" means you can't camp here.
3. No fishing.	"No fishing" means it's forbidden to fish here/in this river/pond.
4. No parking.	"No parking" means you mustn't park (your car) here.
5. No skateboarding.	"No skateboarding" means you're not allowed to skateboard here.
6. No overtaking.	"No overtaking" means you can't/mustn't overtake other cars here.
7. No cycling.	"No cycling" means it's forbidden to cycle here/on this road.
8. No riding.	"No riding" means you're not allowed to ride (a/your horse) here.

6

It was June, and John was already looking forward to going on holiday. His parents wanted to spend three weeks at the seaside again, but John was not keen on lying on the beach in the sun. He preferred skateboarding to swimming in the sea. He was not very good at swimming. There was no chance of staying at home while his parents were on holiday, so John asked his father if he could take his skateboard with him. At first his father was against allowing John to take such a big thing in the car with them, but finally John succeeded in persuading his mother to talk to his father. At last John's dad agreed to let John take his skateboard. ...

Test

1. She prefers roller-skating to skateboarding.
2. Singing is one of my hobbies.
3. I enjoy learning English.
4. She succeeded in passing her exam.
5. We're not used to learning ten new English words a day.
6. It's no use asking him. He doesn't know the answer.

7. Instead of waiting we should leave right away.
8. She's looking forward to getting an e-mail from her pen-friend.
9. "No, I'm not at all interested in meeting you at the disco!"
10. They love eating fish and chips.

Die modalen Hilfsverben 11

1

1. had to — 2. Must we/Do we have to do; must/do — 3. mustn't — 4. have to; needn't — 5. have to — 6. have to — 7. have to — 8. had to — 9. have to — 10. need not/needn't

2

1. mustn't — 2. needn't — 3. mustn't — 4. needn't — 5. needn't — 6. mustn't — 7. needn't — 8. mustn't — 9. mustn't — 10. needn't

3

1. be able to — 2. be able to — 3. could — 4. been able to — 5. couldn't — 6. Are you able to; I won't be able to — 7. would you be able to — 8. was only able to — 9. be able to — 10. can't

4

1. You: May we stroke the goats, please?
2. Girl: Yes of course. You are allowed to stroke all the animals in this part of the zoo.
3. You: My friend wants to know if it is allowed to feed the monkeys.
4. Girl: Of course you may. But you are only allowed to feed them with food you buy here.
5. You: My friend says that in Hamburg we were allowed to feed them our own peanuts.
6. Girl: I'm afraid you may not feed your own food to the animals here.
7. You: OK, thank you. If the weather is good tomorrow, I might come again with a few friends.

5

1. Shall — 2. shouldn't; ought — 3. Shall — 4. oughtn't — 5. shall — 6. Shouldn't — 7. ought — 8. Shall — 9. oughtn't — 10. should — 11. oughtn't — 12. should

6

"What shall we do at the weekend?"
"Let's have a barbecue in the garden. We can invite all our friends: Tania, Paul, Melissa, Jason, Liza."
"Good idea! Shall I phone them or will you?"
"I expect I'll/will see most of them at the youth club tomorrow. Will Maria be back from Spain by the weekend?"
"I'm not sure. Shall we write her a note?"
"Will you do that? I won't have time. But what shall/will we do if it rains?"
"We'll/will have the barbecue in Farmer Jones's old barn. He won't mind."
"Shall we ask him if we can use the barn even if the weather is fine? It would be even better than a barbecue in the garden."
"Good idea. We'll/will have a wonderful time!"

7

1.	Mr Sykes:	"Come in, John. Won't you take your coat off?"
2.	John:	"Would you mind if I kept it on, sir? I'm feeling a bit cold."
3.	Mr Sykes:	"No problem. Would you like something to drink? A cup of tea or coffee?
4.		Or would you rather have a glass of water?"
5.	John:	"I wouldn't mind a cup of coffee, sir. If it's no trouble."
6.	Mr Sykes:	"No trouble at all. *(he picks up the phone)* Jenny – will/would you make us two cups of coffee, please?
7.		The coffee won't be long, John.
8.		While we're waiting, I'll/will ask you a few questions."
9.	John:	"I'll/will try to answer them, sir."
10.	Mr Sykes:	"I wouldn't be too nervous if I were you! They won't be too difficult for you!"

8

When I see this sign …
At this sign …

1. … I should stop and give way at the major road ahead. I may not/mustn't drive straight across – even slowly – because there may be a car coming.
2. … I should drive carefully and watch out for wild animals. I oughtn't to/shouldn't use my headlights full on/I ought to/should dip my headlights because there might be a deer or a fox on the road, and animals stop when they can't see anything/when they are blinded by headlights.
3. … I should drive slowly up to the level crossing and look left and right before I cross. There may/might be a train coming. After the first train has passed I must

still be careful because there may/might be a second train coming from the other direction.

4. … I can't/mustn't turn right. I must/may go straight on or turn left, but I needn't slow down.
5. … I mustn't overtake other vehicles. There may be a dangerous bend ahead, or there might be a narrow bridge. I should drive more slowly and carefully and I shouldn't take extra risks. There is no overtaking on this part of the road.
6. … I must slow down to 30 mph. I mustn't/shouldn't/oughtn't to drive faster when I see this sign because the maximum speed limit is 30 miles per hour. The road may pass through a town, village or past a school, and there may be more pedestrians and children on the road.
7. … I should not be surprised if I hear sudden loud aircraft noises. I shouldn't park on the road near the runways because if a plane crashes it might hit my car. I needn't drive slowly.
8. … there is a river bank, canal or quayside at the end of the road or beside the road. I must drive carefully because there is often mist or fog near water, and I may/might fall into the river or canal. I must not forget to put the handbrake on / I shouldn't park too close to the edge/I shouldn't park here unless I put the handbrake on.

Test

In the street outside the school playground, a pupil is practising skateboarding. A teacher comes round a corner and nearly falls over the pupil.

1. "Be careful! Why **can't** you watch where you're going? You nearly knocked me over!
2. Don't you know that you **mustn't** use a skateboard in the playground?"
3. "I'm sorry. And you **needn't** shout at me. I'm outside the playground.
4. And this is a play street. You **ought** to know that. You're a teacher!"
5. "All right. But you **should** keep your eyes open in future."
6. "Keep my eyes open? You came round a corner! I **couldn't** see you!"

Sonja has lost her keys. She asks her brother if he has seen them.

7. "I've no idea where they are. They **might** be anywhere!
8. **Shall** I help you look for them?"
9. "Thanks. They **must** be somewhere here in my room."
10. "There they are! On your desk! Right in front of your nose. **May** I make a suggestion, Sis?" – "What?" – "Get yourself some new glasses." She throws a book at him. "Ouch!"

12 Die indirekte Rede

1

1. Our teacher **had told** us **to keep** our hand baggage with us at all times and **not to leave** anything on the plane.
2. A voice over the loudspeakers **requested** us **to report** any unattended bags or suitcases and **not to touch** them.
3. The voice over the loudspeakers **was ordering** us **not to panic** but **to leave** the baggage area quietly.
4. The voice also **asked** us **to take** all our personal baggage with us.
5. Our teacher **told** us **to leave** the baggage hall without it.
6. The voice of the loudspeaker **invited** us **to have** a cup of tea and a cake at the airport's expense.
7. Again the loudspeakers **warned** us **not to get** too close to the building and **to stay** away from the windows and glass doors.
8. Finally we **were requested to return** to the baggage hall and **collect** our suitcases.

2

1. Our teacher told us not to wander about. — 2. At the check-in counter the stewardess requested/asked us to put our baggage on the scales. — 3. The passport officer asked/ordered me/us to show him my/our passport(s). — 4. The assistant in the duty-free shop asked me to show him/her my boarding pass. — 5. The stewardess requested/asked passengers in seats 1–40 to board now. — 6. The steward told all passengers to fasten their seat-belts for take-off. — 7. The captain asked us to listen carefully to the safety instructions. — 8. The stewardess warned/told us not to smoke in the toilets.

3

1. The girl said (that) she went to school in London now, but (that she) had gone to school in Scotland for two years. — 2. My teacher says (that) my pronunciation is good and that I can understand a lot of English. — 3. The young woman said (that) he had phoned her hotel after she had left. — 4. He says (that) he has no idea what I am talking about and that he has never seen me before. — 5. The guests told him (that) they were staying at the hotel for a week and so far had been enjoying their stay. — 6. She tells me (that) she wants to become an airline pilot so she has to do well at school. — 7. The girls said (that) they had seen him yesterday and that he had been standing in the school playground. — 8. Our young African visitor told us (that) his grandmother had never seen the sea. — 9. He said (that) Helena knew the answer but wouldn't tell him. — 10. My French friend Jean says (that) Jim and Vera

speak French very well because they've been living in France since 1990. — 11. She told us (that) she had been having a bath when the phone had rung.

4

REPORT OF LOST ITEM

The owner said she **had lost** her rucksack at Victoria Station. She said she **had taken** it off outside the bank at the station before she **had gone** into the bank. The owner said that a friend **had been looking** after the rucksack but that he **had been talking** to some other people and **did not remember** if anyone **had taken** the rucksack by mistake. The two young people from Germany said they **were** not sure where they **were staying** but that they **would ring** us later.

5

1. My friend said we should take a bus because it would be quicker. — 2. The driver told the girl (that) she could sit in the front of the car and that she did not have to sit in the back. — 3. John said (that) his friends had not been able to help him because they had not had time. — 4. My friend's mother told me (that) I had to go or I would miss my train. — 5. The girl said (that) she would like to talk to my brother if she might. — 6. My friend said she ought to ask her mother if she could come with me. — 7. John told me (that) his sister could not come to my party on Saturday because she was going to London. — 8. The guide said (that) it was going to rain and that we should take our raincoats. — 9. Dad told us (that) it might be too cold for a barbecue in the garden but suggested (that) we could have it on the balcony.

6

1. She asked me what time it was. — 2. He asked her if she was English. — 3. She asked them if they had been there. — 4. He asked us if we had phoned Phil. — 5. She wondered when the film started. — 6. He asked me how much money we had got. — 7. She asked him if he had seen Penny yesterday/the day before. — 8. He wanted to know if the sun was shining. — 9. She asked me where I had been born. — 10. He wondered whether/if there was anybody there. — 11. He asked his friend how much he earned. — 12. She wanted to know whether/if Paul had phoned. — 13. He asked her if she had ever eaten lamb. — 14. She asked us where we had gone after we had left school. — 15. She asked them what they would like to drink.

7

1. The inspector wants to know where you were at midnight. — 2. He wants you to tell him what your friend's name is and where she lives. — 3. He says you were seen in Mannheim at 10 pm yesterday and asks how you got to Stuttgart so quickly. —

4. "I took the ICE at a quarter past ten and arrived in Stuttgart at half past eleven." — 5. The inspector is asking how you got to your friend's flat so quickly. — 6. "I took a taxi." — 7. He wants to know how much you paid for the taxi. — 8. "I don't know. I've forgotten." — 9. "Why did/have you come to Stuttgart?" — 10. "I want/wanted to plan another burglary with some friends."

8

1. The young man suggested going for a ride on his motor-bike.
2. The girl suggested going to the cinema.
3. One driver suggested that the other driver should go back to driving school.
4. Our teacher suggested that we should do exercise 6 again.
5. The tourist suggested going to a museum.
6. The waitress (at the snack-bar) suggested that the boys and girls/young people should have hamburgers and chips.

9

1. They asked me how long I had been living here. — 2. John wanted to know if my sister was going to the youth club tonight. — 3. Jim and Barbara said they had gone to the disco the previous day/the day before. — 4. They said they were going on holiday next month. — 5. He said he was going to London the following month. — 6. He/She said his/her mother was going to buy a new car that week. — 7. He/she said (that) his/her class test was tomorrow. — 8. He/she said (that) John had told him/her (that) he lived here. — 9. He/she said (that) John had told him/her (that) he lived in that street. — 10. They said (that) they had seen Paul and Jean a few days before/ago.

Test

Die Konjunktion *that* wird in der gesprochenen Sprache meist weggelassen.

1. My mother told me **to be polite** to my host family.
2. And my father warned me **not to go to discos** too often.
3. They asked me **not to forget to phone them** when I arrived.
4. My father said **he hoped (that) I would have a good time**.
5. My mother told me (that) she had written to my host family /you. Did you get her letter? - Yes, we got it last week.
6. She said **she hoped (that) you could understand her English**. - It was quite good, actually.
7. My parents said **(that) they would like to visit me in England**.
8. My mother wanted to know **if/whether it/that would be possible**.
9. My father asked **if/whether there was an interesting** leisure-time programme.

10. And my mother never stops worrying about me! She wondered when we would arrive in London and said (that) she hoped it wouldn't be too late in the evening! Aren't parents the absolute end!

Relativsätze 13

1

a) 1. A thermometer is a device which tells the temperature. — 2. A bus-driver is a person who drives a bus. — 3. A discjockey is a person who plays CDs and records at a disco. — 4. A plane/An aircraft is a vehicle which has wings. — 5. A teacher is a man or woman who works in a school. — 6. A road sign is a sign that tells drivers what to do. — 7. A pupil is a boy or girl who goes to school. — 8. A lemon is a yellow fruit which is very sour. — 9. An umbrella is a small, portable roof which keeps out the rain.

b) 1. A passport is a document (which/that) you need when you go abroad. — 2. Chewing gum is something (which/that) you can chew. — 3. A bus is a vehicle which/that takes people to work or school. — 4. A cat is an animal which/that can catch mice. — 5. An explorer is a person who/that explores unknown countries or regions. — 6. A walkman is a device which/that plays music while you are walking. — 7. Students are people who/that go to college or university. — 8. A snowboard is something (which/that) you can use in the mountains in winter, like skis. — 9. Rollerskates are things with wheels (which/that) you put on your feet. You can then "roll" along the ground very quickly. — 10. A ghost is something which/that lives in an empty castle or house/something which/that few people believe in.

2

1. Prince Charles, who is the son of the Queen, has two sons.
2. The blackbird, which lives in trees, has red legs.
3. John Evans, who works in a coal mine, speaks Welsh.
4. The Mini, which is a small two-door car, is still very popular.
5. English, which is spoken everywhere, is a world language.
6. Hamburg, which is a city in Germany, is a large port.
7. Flying doctors, who help sick people, work in Australia.
8. Coal, which is a black mineral, burns very well.
9. John Wayne, who was a film-star, could ride a horse.
10. Bristol, which was once a large port, is west of London.

3

Bestimmende Relativsätze:

A teenager who stole a car was arrested in Brighton. — The car which he stole was a blue Morris 1100 that belonged to Ms Jane Campbell. — The policemen who followed the stolen car … are the same men who stopped two joyriders last month. The police car which they were driving … — a busy road that is used by thousands of cars. — … the car that was following him … — … the Morris 1100 which Wilkinson had stolen ran out of petrol.

Nicht-bestimmende Relativsätze:

James Wilkinson, who lives at 69, High Street, Thornton Heath, is only 16. — Ms Jane Campbell, who also lives in Thornton Heath. — James broke into the car, which was parked outside Ms Campbell's house, … — He was unable to steal the radio, which was firmly fixed to the dashboard, … — PC Alfred Frazer, who lives in Warlingham. — … the A23, which is a busy road, … — The policemen, who could see that the driver was very young, did not wish to frighten the thief, who was driving at about 65 mph, … — … the crew of another police car, which had been waiting …, caught him.

4

Come to Tenby for a seaside holiday which/that is different!

People who/that enjoy seaside holidays will love Tenby. This small seaside town in South Wales, which has two wonderful sandy beaches, is also famous for the castle which/that stands at the top of the town between the two bays. Tenby is an ideal place for young people who/that want to do more than lie on the beach. There are many interesting paths which/that follow the rocky coastline, and for those of you who/that are not good walkers, there are plenty of places which/that are worth visiting in the town itself. There are boat trips to the small island of Caldy, which has a lighthouse and a Roman Catholic monastery. Jean Smith, who has been coming to Tenby regularly for over 50 years, says: "Tenby is a place which/that attracts all kinds of people, old (like me) and young (like my granddaughter), who is here with me this year."

5

(Achte auch auf die Kommas!)

1. This is the man who/that lives in the flat above ours.
2. Do you like ice-cream which/that tastes like toffee?
3. John Brown, who lives next door, is a good friend of mine. *or:* John Brown, who is a good friend of mine, lives next door.
4. She is wearing a long skirt which/that is very pretty.
5. The clothes which/that she buys in Paris are expensive.
6. My girlfriend Alison, who is 19, lives in Cleversulz-bach. *or:* My girlfriend Alison, who lives in Cleversulzbach, is 19.

7. This is the bus that/which goes to Euston Station.
8. Here are the shoes that/which cost me £60.
9. When did you see the man that/who stole my car?
10. This coffee, which smells very fresh, comes all the way from Kenya.

6

The place I went to for my summer holidays last year was a little village which/that is difficult to find on most maps of Scotland but a place you will easily find on a map of Canada: Calgary on the Island of Mull, which is off the west coast of Scotland. The Canadian town which/that is called Calgary was originally a small fort the Canadian Mounted Police founded in 1875 as Fort Brisebois, a French name few of the policemen could pronounce correctly. The fort was renamed Calgary, which means "clear running water" in Gaelic, by Colonel James F. Macleod, who came from the Island of Mull. The year in which the fort was renamed was 1876. The small hotel we stayed at had a fine view of the bay, which, with its blue sea and pure white sand, was ideal for bathing.

7

1. The school project we did was about London in the 19th century. — 2. The teacher who helped us collect material was Mr Peters. — 3. Some of the material we collected was very interesting. — 4. Anne Harrap, who I was working on the project with, is a good friend of mine. — 5. Our part of the project was something we didn't know much about: the London Underground! — 6. The first part of the London Underground, which is still the biggest underground network in the world, opened in 1863. — 7. Even in those days the streets which connected the suburbs of West London with the banks and offices of the City were overcrowded. — 8. This first underground railway, which many "commuters" used, was called the Metropolitan Railway. — 9. The name it was given was taken over by underground railways all over the world. — 10. The Paris and Moscow "Metros", which are used by millions each day, are both named after it. — 11. The first real "tube" railway (which) electric trains were used on was built in 1890. — At the end of the 19th century there were many miles of underground lines, which most people preferred to the horse buses above ground. — Londoners are proud of their Underground. But the man who did most to start up the system was an American. — 14. Charles Tyson Yerkes, who had made a fortune in the USA, was the man Londoners should be grateful to for their Underground. — 15. It was he who insisted on electric trains instead of steam engines in the early days. — 16. The Glasgow Underground, which was for many years the only other "Metro" in Britain, had a very small, very dirty circular line with steam trains which lasted until the 1930s!

8

1. The new Arrow sports car, which is made in Coventry, won a rally which/that was organized by the Automobile Club of Scotland. — 2. A boy of 16 who built his own plane flew 500 metres before crashing into a car which/that was parked in the middle of a field. — 3. Melissa Ryman, who lives in London, will swim for England at the European championships, which begin next week in Paris. — 4. The open-air concert which/that was cancelled last week will take place next week at Folly Farm, which is near Oxford. — 5. The first British spacecraft "Britannia I", which will be launched next month, will carry four astronauts who/that were chosen from over 1000 applicants. — 6. The/A computer which/that was developed by an Irish company will be sold by Eurocomp, which has its headquarters in Dublin.

9

1. James Watt was an inventor whose steam engine revolutionized industry.
2. Watt was born in Scotland, the capital of which is Edinburgh.
3. This is the rare XL 320 sports car, only 200 of which were built.
4. The man whose car had been stolen was very angry.
5. The Rolling Stones, whose songs have been best sellers since the 60s, are still together.
6. The company the collapse of which was forecast months ago is still doing well.
7. Mr Smith(,) whose son won the prize(,) was very happy.
8. The car the door of which was damaged belonged to Mr Granger.
9. The man whose daughter won the prize was very happy.
10. The villages whose streets were flooded were cut off.

Test

Der Gedankenstrich (–) bedeutet, man kann das Relativpronomen auch weglassen, da es Objekt im notwendigen Relativsatz ist.

1. The house in **which** we live was built in 1906.
2. Mr Aloysius Prang, **who** built it**,** was a rather eccentric man.
3. The materials **which/that/–** he used were very modern at the time: concrete and steel girders.
4. But the brickwork on the front of the house, **which** looks like most houses built in 1906, is only painted on the concrete!
5. Few people look twice at our house, **which** my parents bought five years ago.
6. But a year ago an architect **who/that** had heard about the house visited us.
7. He told us he had heard about a house the front of **which** was painted to look like brick.
8. He was writing a book about architects **whose** ideas had been ahead of their time.

9 He said that Aloysius Prang, whose house we were living in, had been one of them

10. So now our house is famous! There is a long article about our house in the book by the young architect who/whom /– we talked to that day.

Die Pronomen 14

1

Yesterday we went shopping by bus. The bus was late. When it arrived, we got on. The bus-driver asked us where we wanted to go. I said: "Tooting Station, please" and she said: "Tooting, too." He smiled and said: "Two to Tooting!" The people in the bus heard him. They laughed at his little joke. We thought they were very silly. We didn't look at them. We gave him the money. He took the money and gave us our tickets and our change. He gave me 5p change and gave her 45p. My ticket said: 45p. Mary looked at it, too. Then she looked at me and I looked at her. "Excuse me," I said to the driver. "You've given her the wrong change. She gave you a pound coin and it's only 45p to Tooting Station. You only gave her 45p change instead of 55p." He gave her another 10p. He was not smiling now. All the other people in the bus were looking at him. "He's given one of them the wrong change!" said an old man. We smiled at him. "I'm going to Tooting, too!" he said. This time everybody laughed – except the bus driver, of course!

2

"I've lost my keys, Dad. Can you help me to find them?"
"Weren't they on the table in the hall this morning?"
"No, those were Mum's keys. I gave them to Mum. My keys were in my jacket pocket, but I can't find my jacket. Have you seen it?"
"Your old jeans jacket? I think Mum gave it away this morning."
"Gave my jacket away? It was my favourite jeans jacket. I wore it almost every day – and it wasn't old. Only a year or two, anyway."
"There were some people at the door this morning. They were collecting old clothes for the Red Cross. I think Mum gave them your jacket – and a few of my old clothes, too."
"But surely Mum looked in the pockets before she gave the things away!"
"I'm not sure, Carol. By the way, have you seen my old black trousers? They were in the bedroom but now I can't find them. There was a £20 note in the back pocket! Where's Mum, anyway. Just wait till I see her! I'll give her a boot in the head if she's given my trousers away!"

3

1 "She is from London. I understand her well." – "Do you know where she lives?"
2. "Do they come from Berlin?" – "No, they come from Cologne. I know them well." – "Do you know where they live?"
3. "She is in my class. I see her every day."
4. "I think these books are good. You can buy them everywhere."
5. "Have you seen Ken and Tom?" – "Yes, I saw them in the playground. They were playing football."

4

Am besten prüfst du deine Antworten „von oben nach unten"! Wir haben die wahrscheinlichsten Kombinationen aufgelistet. Deine zehn Sätze müssten dabei sein. Wenn nicht, kannst du im Zweifelsfall deine(n) Lehrer(in) fragen. Er/Sie wird sich sicher über dein zusätzliches Engagement im Englischen freuen!

My friend Brian bought a new CD / some sweets / a magazine for his friend Jack / for me.
My friend Brian bought me / her brother / us / them / my friend Jack a new CD.
My friend Brian gave a new CD / some sweets / it / them / a magazine / a letter to us / to his sister.
My friend Brian gave me / us / them /my friend Jack a new CD.
My friend Brian sent a letter / a magazine to us / to his sister.
My friend Brian sent me / us / them /her brother / my friend Jack a new CD / a postcard from France.
My friend Brian lent a new CD / a magazine / it / them to us / to his sister.
My friend Brian lent her brother / me / us / them / my friend Jack a new CD.

I bought a new CD / some sweets / a magazine for his friend Jack.
I bought her brother / them / my friend Jack a new CD.
I gave a new CD / some sweets / it / them / a magazine to his sister.
I gave her brother / them / my friend Jack a new CD.
I sent a letter / a magazine to us / to his sister.
I sent her brother / them /my friend Jack a new CD / a postcard from France.
I lent a new CD / a magazine / it / them to his sister.
I lent her brother / them / my friend Jack a new CD.

Her mum bought a new CD / it / them / some sweets / a magazine for his friend Jack / for me.
Her mum bought her brother / me / us / them / my friend Jack a new CD.
Her mum gave a new CD / some sweets / a magazine / a letter to us / to his sister.

Her mum gave her brother / me / us / them / my friend Jack a new CD.
Her mum sent a letter / a magazine to us / to his sister.
Her mum sent me / us / them /her brother / my friend Jack a new CD / a postcard from France.
Her mum lent a new CD / a magazine / it / them to us / to his sister.
Her mum lent her brother / me / us / them / my friend Jack a new CD.

You bought a new CD / it / them / some sweets / a magazine for me / for his friend Jack.
You bought her brother / me / us / them / my friend Jack a new CD.
You gave a new CD / some sweets / a magazine / it / them to us / to his sister.
You gave me / her brother / them / my friend Jack a new CD.
You sent a letter / a magazine / some sweets to us / to his sister.

You sent her brother / me / us / them / my friend Jack a new CD / a postcard from France.
You lent a new CD / a magazine / it / them to us / to his sister.
You lent her brother / me / us / / them / my friend Jack a new CD.

We bought a new CD / some sweets / a magazine for his friend Jack.
We bought her brother / them / my friend Jack a new CD.
We gave a new CD / some sweets / it / them / a magazine to his sister.
We gave her brother / them / my friend Jack a new CD.
We sent a letter / a magazine / some sweets to his sister.
We sent her brother / them / my friend Jack a new CD / a postcard from France.
We lent a new CD / a magazine / it / them to his sister.
We lent her brother / them / my friend Jack a new CD.

5

1. I gave him the money.
2. She sent a letter to her.
3. She bought them an ice-cream.
4. He/She gave us a test yesterday.
5. We sent it to them by airmail.
6. He gave it them.
7. He bought them for her last year.
8. They showed them (to) us/us them.
9. Can she lend them (to) her/her them?

6

1. "I always do my homework myself. Nobody helps me."
   "What about your sister? Does she do her homework herself?"
   "Well, she's younger than me. Sometimes my father helps her."
2. Some of the girls in my class make their clothes themselves. I've tried making my own clothes, but when I put them on and look at myself in a mirror, I hope that other people won't laugh at me when they see me!"
3. "I'm thirsty," he asked me. "Can I get myself a glass of orange juice?"
   "Of course!" I said. "Help yourself!" So he poured himself a glass of orange juice.
   "Shall I pour a glass for you?" he asked me and my brother.
   "No, thanks," I said. "We can pour ourselves a glass when we're thirsty."
4. We have a big garden, so we grow a lot of our own food ourselves. Our neighbours have tried growing their food themselves, but they only have a small garden.
5. My cat is very clever. When it's hungry, it goes into the kitchen and gets itself something to eat. The box of cat food is on the floor. The cat knocks it over. Some bits of food fall out of it, and the cat eats them.

7

Lösungswörter in Klammern gelten als „weniger wahrscheinlich" richtige Lösungen!
"I was in London last week." – "We were in London ourselves. We didn't see you there." – "Well, London itself is a big city, isn't it? I went on a tour of Buckingham Palace. It was a very expensive tour, so we had to pay for our tickets ourselves. Prince Charles himself was the tour guide! The rooms themselves were very interesting, but I wanted to see the Queen herself/(myself). There was a door with a sign 'NO ENTRY'. When nobody was looking, I opened the door and walked right into the private rooms of the Royal Family itself/(themselves)! They themselves live right in the middle of the Palace itself. There was nobody about, so I had to find the Queen's living-room myself. At last I found it – and there was Her Majesty herself, sitting in an armchair and reading a newspaper." – "I don't believe you! You made that story up yourself!" – "You're right. But both of you almost believed my story yourselves, didn't you?"

8

1. "Hi, Karen. Have you met my brother Vincent?" – "Oh yes. Vincent and I have known one another/each other for years."
2. Some of my friends are not very good at English. So we sometimes meet after school and help each other/one another with our homework.
3. A farmer in our village had too many apples last year. He put a lot of apples in a box beside the road with a sign on it: FREE APPLES. HELP YOURSELVES / (YOURSELF). So we helped ourselves.

4. She was too big for her old bike, so she bought **herself** a new one.
5. I hadn't seen my cousin for six years. When we met again last week, we hardly recognised **each other/one another**.
6. We went to the open-air concert in the afternoon and watched it again on TV in the evening. We saw **ourselves** in the crowd.
7. "They never think about other people. They are selfish. They only think about **themselves**." – "I hate selfish people! I think everybody should help **each other/ one another**."
8. "I painted that picture of the river **myself**. Do you like it?" – "The picture **itself** is OK, but I don't like the colours much!"
9. "I grew up in London. Have you ever been to London **yourself**?" – "No. Only to London Airport, not to London **itself**."
10. Nobody can help us. We'll have to do it **ourselves**.
11. "Shall I tell Mum and Dad that I broke your window, Mrs Smith?" – "No, John. I'll tell your parents **myself**."
12. "Did I see you and Vera talking to **each other /one another** at the party?" – "That's right. She didn't know many people **herself**. In fact she told me she had come to the party by **herself**."

9

1. "Whose bike is that? Is it **yours**?" – "No, it isn't **mine**. I didn't bring **mine** to school today. Ask Peter – I think it's **his**."
2. *(After the party)* "Where did you put your coats?" – "We put **ours** on the bed. I think Barbara and Ken put **theirs** on the bed, too."
3. "Have you seen my English books, Sheila?" – "No, Helen. These are my books. Where did you leave **yours**?" – "I left them here, on the table, right next to **yours**." – "Oh dear! Tania thought those books were **hers**. She put them in her bag and went home, I think." – "Just a minute, Sheila. There's a bag over there. I think it's **Tania's/hers**. She must still be here. I'll find her and ask her about the books."

10

1. "That must be Mr Jones's car over there." – "No. I think it's **Mr Smith's**."
2. "It wasn't my mistake. It was **our headmaster's**: he ordered the wrong books."
3. "Is that your house?" – "No, that's **the Browns'**. **Ours** is next door."
4. "Are those your glasses?" – "No, I'm wearing **mine**. They must be **Mum's**."
5. "Do you know Alice and Paul Smith?" – "Of course. They're good friends of **ours**."

Test

1. Mum: Victor? Kenneth? What's all that shouting about? What are **you** doing?
2. Victor: Ken's playing with my game-boy! Give it **me** back!
3. Kenneth: It's not your game-boy, Vic. It's **mine**!
   Mum: So whose game-boy is this one under the table?
4. Kenneth: Oh! Sorry, Vic. This one belongs **to me**. I must have dropped it …
   Mum: Anyway, didn't you two want to go surfing on the Internet this afternoon with Chris and Bonzo?
5. Kenneth: No, they're no friends of **ours**!
   Mum: Well, I saw their mother at the supermarket this morning. She said you two had invited them to come round here after school to try out your new computer.
   Victor: Are you sure it was Chris and Bonzo's mother? Mrs Brown from Number 193?
6. Mum: Of course I'm sure. I spoke to her **myself**.
7. Kenneth: We didn't invite them, Mum. They must have invited **themselves**!
8. Mum: What's wrong? Don't you like them? I thought all the boys and girls in your class liked **each other**.
9. Victor: Most of us do, Mum, and Bonzo **himself** is OK. But nobody likes Chris Brown much.

Stressfreies Lernen und bessere Noten mit dem Aktiv-Lernprogramm

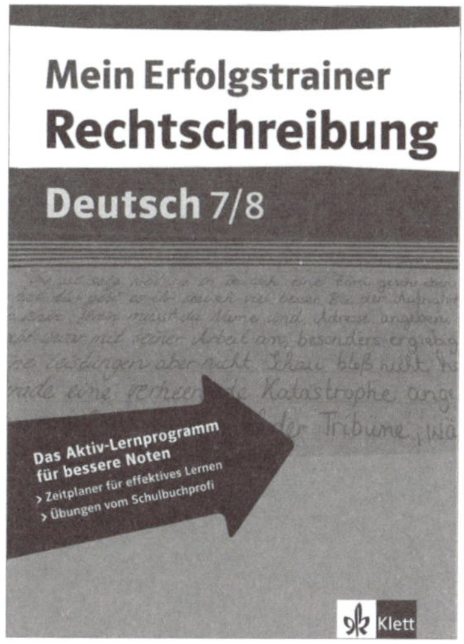

Mein Erfolgstrainer
Textaufgaben
5. Schuljahr
ISBN 978-3-12-927129-2
Preis: 13,95 €

Mein Erfolgstrainer
Rechtschreibung
5./6. Schuljahr
ISBN 978-3-12-927133-9
Preis: 13,95 €

Mein Erfolgstrainer
Rechtschreibung
9./10. Schuljahr
ISBN 978-3-12-927135-3
Preis: 13,95 €

Mein Erfolgstrainer
Englische Grammatik
7./8. Schuljahr
ISBN 978-3-12-927137-7
Preis: 13,95 €

Mein Erfolgstrainer
Textaufgaben
6.–8. Schuljahr
ISBN 978-3-12-927132-2
Preis: 13,95 €

Mein Erfolgstrainer
Rechtschreibung
7./8. Schuljahr
ISBN 978-3-12-927134-6
Preis: 13,95 €

Mein Erfolgstrainer
Englische Grammatik
5./6. Schuljahr
ISBN 978-3-12-927136-0
Preis: 13,95 €

Mein Erfolgstrainer
Englische Grammatik
9./10. Schuljahr
ISBN 978-3-12-927138-4
Preis: 13,95 €

Diese und weitere Klett-Lernhilfen sind im Buchhandel erhältlich.

Informationen finden Sie unter **www.klett.de**

Klett Lernen und Wissen, Postfach 10 26 45, 70022 Stuttgart
Telefon 0180 · 255 38 82, Telefax 0180 · 255 38 83